A Comprehensive Illustrated Manual on the
Joyful Art of Cunnilingus

Oral Caress

The Loving Guide to Exciting
A Woman

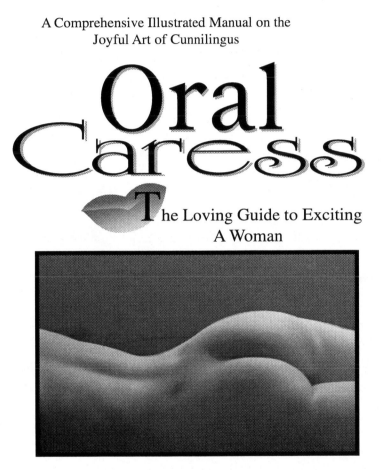

ROBERT W. BIRCH, Ph.D., FAACS
Psychologist, Marital Therapist
and
Certified Sex Therapist

ORAL CARESS: The *LOVING* Guide to Exciting a Woman
ISBN: 1-57074-307-X

Publisher: PEC Publications

Manufactured in the United States of America

PEC Publications
28 W. Henderson Road
Columbus, Ohio 43214-2628
(614) 261-9343
(614) 261-8280 FAX

Library of Congress Cataloging-in-Publication Data *Birch, Robert W.*

Oral Caress
1. Sexuality   2. Women - Sexual Behavior   3. Marriage
4. Relationships

Sexual acts portrayed are simulations by consenting adults 21 years of age or
older. Records are maintained by the author. The publisher of LIBIDO
gratiously consented to the use of their statement concerning women and
pornography. The use of this statement does not imply any association with
the editorial or publishing staff of LIBIDO, nor their endorsement of this
book.

This book contains practices that are not considered to be "safe sex." The
author is not responsible for the sexual conduct or misconduct of the readers.
Readers, however, are reminded to practice safe sex and, if they are uncertain
about what is safe, are advised to consult their physician.

Sexism, not sex, degrades women. The publishers believe that adults should be free to read about sex and view sexual images without reprecussions from thought-police of any stripe. To lump all sexual images together as degrading to women implies that women do not enjoy sex, that they don't engage in it of their own volition, and that something pleasurable to men must necessarily be repugnant to women. This attitude is patronizing to women.

Statement by the editors of

LIBIDO, The Journal of Sex and Sensibility

ACKNOWLEDGEMENTS

Appreciation is expressed to **Dr. Judith Seifer**, President of the American Association of Sex Educators, Counselors and Therapists, who took time from her busy schedule to read and comment on my manuscript. Thanks Judy for your enthusiasm. **Cynthia Lief Ruberg**, a colleague and AASECT Certified Sex Counselor deserves special recognition. On an ongoing basis, Cindy contributed both personal thoughts and professional insights. Warm thanks are also extended to **Dr. Beverly Whipple** and to **Dr. Roger Libby,** both of whom were generous in offering suggestions and comments. Professional sexologist are such a gratious and giving lot.

Appreciation is also expressed to **Melissa Matthews** a Women's Studies major and, at present, a graduate student in Counseling. Melissa added a valuable woman's perspective, and offered ongoing encouragement. Comments by **Liz Williams**, Clinical Social Worker and sexuality educator, were also quite helpful.

As the manuscript neared completion, **Shari Stoner** sat patiently and carefully read material that had already been read and re-read. With each of Shari's readings she inevitably found typographical errors that others had missed. **Cindy Kingery** added invaluable technical advice, without which publication would have been much more difficult.

The quality of this book has been greatly enhanced by the sensual artistry of photographer **Pete Nitschke**. I very much appreciate his significant contribution, and I am sure that I am not alone in finding the erotic images he presents quite pleasing. Thanks also to the folks at PHE, Inc. (especially **Cyndi Horner**) for help with finding appropriate illustrations.

How could I not acknowledge the wonderful sense of freedom and openness of those who have graciously shared their photographic images with us. These were not pornographic exhibits, but rather the joyful celebration of the natural beauty of human sexuality. Thank you! Thank you for reminding us that there is no shame in being nude nor in being sexual.

Finally, behind many male authors there is an understanding wife. Such a wonderfully patient woman has been there for me, tolerating my periodic physical and emotional absence as I obsessed over my manuscript. Her encouragement and support has never wavered, and I am most grateful to have **Sue** in my life.

*All photographs, unless otherwise noted,
are by Pete Nitschke*

Appreciation is expressed to
all the photographers and their models.
Photo credits appear at back of book.

TABLE OF CONTENTS

INTRODUCTION

The author's original purpose was to present a <u>comprehensive educational</u> manual on the art of orally stimulating a woman. In reviewing a very early draft of this book, Dr. Roger Libby, teacher, author, humorist and sex therapist, wrote me, stating "The manuscript has some humor, but it is predominately educational. I would approach it more wildly, rather than so cautiously. Make it more 'tongue in cheeks'!" It remains important to me to transmit factual and educational information, but, with the recommended "wildness" in mind, I will attempt to do so in a fun way. After all, l do wish to accurately reflect the playfulness of the popular sexual activity about which I write.

It is well known that heterosexual and bisexual men enjoy orally stimulating women, as do lesbian and bisexual women. In a time when "political correctness" seems of utmost importance, it remains difficult to write a book that is consistently gender-neutral. Therefore, I invite you, the reader, regardless of your gender, preference or sexual orientation, to read this publication as if it had been written specifically for you!! All persuasions are welcome to join in this joyful celebration of oral sex (or, as some prefer, "eating pussy"). If you love going down on a woman and want to learn more, read on. Hopefully you will learn a great deal, and in response to some "tongue in cheeks" humor, my words may bring an occasional smile.

This publication is <u>explicit</u>, both in words and picture, and the naive reader who might have believed this book to be about cats, is likely to find the material unsettling. If you're into raising felines and not into eating pussy, close this book immediately! The material presented is intended to whet the appetites of <u>consenting adults only</u>.

Dr. Libby has suggested that those who finish the book should be given an "oral exam." It is recommended, therefore, that you keep your partner close, so upon completion of your reading she can put you to this final test. Perhaps it should be called the "taste test!"

Bᴇᴛᴛᴇʀ ꜱᴀꜰᴇ ᴛʜᴀɴ ꜱᴏʀʀʏ

Despite the playful nature, I do want to remind you that any unprotected sexual activity with a stranger (or a group of strangers) carries some danger to your health. Care should be taken to avoid high risk situations. This very brief section is certainly not intended to cover all aspects of sexually transmitted disease or the various forms of protection from infection. Those who are sexually active with a variety of partners should educate themselves on how to best minimize their risk. The presence of AIDS and other sexually transmitted diseases in our society does not mean the end of sex. It simply means we need to be careful!

A ᴄᴏɴᴄɪꜱᴇ ᴅɪᴄᴛɪᴏɴᴀʀʏ ᴏꜰ ᴏʀᴀʟ ꜱᴇx

Oral sex, in the more scientific literature, is often referred to as **oral-genital contact**. In the Kinsey reports of the mid 40's, the practice is referred to as **mouth-genital contact**. The term **oragenitalism** was coined by Gershon Legman in 1969 in his book on oral sex, later reprinted in paperback under the title The Intimate Kiss. In the book entitled Sexual Attitudes and Lifestyles, published in England in 1994, the term **orogenital sexual contact** is employed. Elsewhere the term **oral intercourse** finds favor, while **oral manipulation** is used by others. **Fellatio** is the formal term for oral stimulation of a man's penis.

Cunnilingus, the main topic of this book, is the oral stimulation (with lips, mouth and/or tongue) of a woman's genitals (including the lips, the clitoris and clitoral hood, the vaginal opening, and the perineum). Less commonly, oral stimulation of the female genitals has been called **cunnilinctus** or **cunnilinctio**. The terms are derived from the Latin word "cunnus" (meaning "vulva") and "lingus" (meaning "tongue"). Obviously the Latin word "cunnus" is the root of our word "cunt" - a term which should always be used with affection. Of all the labels for female genitals in use today, "cunt" may be one of the oldest. Robert Burchfield, in his magisterial Supplement to the Oxford English Dictionary, demonstrates that the earliest known use in literature occurred in about 1230! That's about 765 years of usage.

In the more popular literature the term **intimate kiss** or the **ultimate kiss** has been used and Dr. Kenneth Ray Stubbs has, in his fun guide to oral sex, referred to the **clitoral kiss**. Dr. Roger Libby, in pseudo-Latin, playfully calls it **clitus lickus**!

Many popular terms for cunnilingus have emerged over the years and a rich library of street language has developed. Most readers will be familiar with the terms **muff diving**, **eating at the Y**, and **tonguing her taco**. **Giving head** and **eating pussy** are quite descriptive and in common usage. One can also, of course, **eat a snatch**. **Quaffing the bearded clam** has been used in the past, and more recently the eater has been called a **clam diver**. **Box lunch**, **fur burger**, and **hair pie** are terms for the tasty target of the muff diver's tongue. **Going down** will sound recent and familiar, with **going south** being a similar but less frequently used expression. To **tip the velvet** and **play the harmonica** are older expressions for cunnilingus. Alan Richter, in his fascinating book The Language of Sexuality, writes that one obscure term, dating back to the Eighteenth century, is **larking**.

Frenching refers to oral stimulation and, in classified personal ads, those describing their sexual interests as "French" or involving the "French culture" are signalling their desire to find horny partners who also delight in oral sex. In French, a cunnilinguist is a **gamahucheur**. In English, a person who performs cunnilingus is formally called a **cunnilictor** or **cunnilinguist**. One who really loves eating pussy is a **cunnophile**. Within the list of street names for one who eats with gusto are **gash eater**, **gash gourmet**, **lap lover**, and **vacuum cleaner**. Finally, one who engages in giving head to a woman may be called a **cake eater**, **cat lapper**, or **clit licker**.

I would like to introduce the term **cunnianorexic** to designate someone who vigorously avoids eating at the Y. This term, which I have coined, combines "cunni" (signifying the object of disdain) and "anorexic" (the medical label for one who refuses to eat). This book is offered as a remedy for those suffering from **cunnianorexia**, a condition we might also call **oraphobia**. Many might argue, however, that this avoidance of cunnilingus is not really a phobia, but rather just "a matter of taste."

Analingus is the "official" term for oral stimulation of the anal region. An **analist** is a person who has eroticized the anal area and engages in fantasies or activities involving this posterior region. In the popular language to **rim** is to circle with one's tongue the anal sphincter (opening to the **dirt track**) of a partner. Other terms that have appeared in writing are **ass blow, cleaning up the kitchen**, and **playing the piano** (reported to be a playful reference to the name of the pianist Rimski-Korsakov). What could be more explicit than the street term **tongue-fuck** - a street term that has been used in connection with inserting the tongue into either the vagina or the anus.

Taking a **trip to the moon** is to travel to the region of the buns. To go **around the world** is to lick and suck the entire genital, perineal, and anal area. The perineum, that area between the vaginal opening and the anal sphincter, has been playfully called the **t'aint**, because it "t'aint" that opening and it "t'aint" that other one either!

Xxx EDUCATION

You might wonder, "Why read a book about giving head to a woman when the XXX-rated adult videos are filled with scenes of cunnilingus?" If you view one of the many "suck and fuck" videos on the

market, you will note that the majority of scenes showing oral sex on a woman involve positions that offer little stimulation to the receiving actress, but provide great camera shots for the voyeuristic home viewer. Whenever you see the eater extend his or her tongue out as far as possible, making only superficial contact, you can generally assume that the director's primary interest is in getting a good view of the woman's spread genital lips. Favoring this "split beaver" shot, the pornographer is operating on the theory that "pink sells!!"

In really good cunnilingus, the giver buries his or her face in the receiver's goodies, blocking the view of the tasty target. The film director would find nothing visually erotic in a shot of a woman lying spread eagle with her eater's head buried deeply between her open thighs. In most videos, therefore, what you get for your viewing fare, are the images of an eater coming in from the side, leaning across the leg furthest from the camera with tongue painfully extended. The lick is so light the woman is not likely to feel much, but on cue, she will squeal, moan and groan as though receiving the ultimate in oral pleasure.

You will notice also that there are many shots of tongue stimulation down around the vaginal opening. This would certainly feel good to most receivers. However, for the majority of women, licking around the vaginal opening is much less effective than lingual caress around the clitoris. If the director of the adult video wants plenty of good shots of the clitoris, this small protuberance cannot be obstructed by the cunnilinguist's tongue. While working well for solitary arousal, fantasy and masturbation, the majority of hard-core productions do not provide good information for the eager student wishing to become an expert at skillfully administering the oral caress.

Adult videos are not without merit, however. They do demonstrate clearly that men, lesbians, and bisexual women really love to stimulate a woman orally. Within these adult videos, you will never see the eater emerge from between a woman's legs gagging and wiping juices from his or her face! Rather, what you see is an abundance of enjoyment on the part of the giver and a wealth of excitement (though probably a bit exaggerated) on the part of the receiver. While these XXX-rated videos may not provide good sex education, they do convey plenty of healthy permission - permission to get on down there and have some great oral fun!

Resource Tip

A major source of adult entertainment is **Adam & Eve,** *P.O. Box 800, Carrboro, NC 27510. Write also to* **The Sexuality Library,** *938 Howard St., Suite 101, San Francisco, CA 94103.*

Some women feel competitive with the young and attractive video performers or are uncomfortable viewing explicit sexual scenes. They may become upset if they discover that their partner enjoys watching porn. Therefore, you must be sure to understand your partner's feelings about explicit material before bringing home a copy of "Debbie Does Everyone." On the other hand, many women enjoy watching skin, experience some excitement, and love seeing their partners become aroused as they watch the flick together. Being anything but jealous, one woman told her partner, "I don't care where you get your appetite, just as long as you come home to eat!

Many women find the general run of the mill porn flicks to be devoid of caring, to be sexist and/or to be degrading to women. With this in mind, Candida Royalle has, according to Time magazine, "...burst into the public eye with her ground-breaking creation of couples' erotica from a woman's point of view." Unlike typical porn, the videos directed to a female audience show a greater emphasis on story line, romance, loving foreplay and realistic sexual encounters (without close-up shots of over-sized penises pounding piston-like into shaved crotches).

Resource Tip

A catalog of Candida Royalle's videos can be obtained by writing to **Femme Distribution**, *588 Broadway, Suite 1110, New York, NY 10012.*

There is another new and different variety of explicit visual material now on the market. These are the adult educational videos that are written, directed, and narrated by professional sexologists, sex educators and sex therapists. The information given is accurate and the graphics realistic, often involving a committed couple who are comfortable being videotaped as they talk openly about their sexuality and as they share their lovemaking behavior with the viewer. The professional narration and the explicit demonstration provide an excellent format for "teaching old dogs new tricks."

Resource Tip

*A good source for instructional self-help videos of superior quality in both professional narration and superb photography is **The Sinclair Institute,** P.O. Box 8865, Chapel Hill, NC 27515. Also, check out the variety of videos available from the **Playboy Catalog,** P.O. Box 809, Itasca, IL 60143. **Focus International,** 1160 East Jericho Turnpike, Suite 15, Huntington, NY 11743, is another excellent resource.*

But is cunnilingus normal?

Since everyone seems to believe that they alone know what is "normal," it becomes a very difficult concept to agree upon. With "normal" being such a subjective word, those who pride themselves on being cunnophiles would unanimously concur that eating at the Y is quite "normal." On the other side of the table, however, those "cunnianorexics" who prudishly pride themselves on avoiding all lustful pleasures of the flesh will quickly label the tonguing of a taco as clearly "abnormal." There are those who would argue that any sexual behavior that could not lead to pregnancy is abnormal and still others would argue that anything that feels good must be "wrong." Procreation, by this logic (or illogic) is good and recreation is bad!

The concept of "good" and "bad" is not the same as the concept of "normal" and "abnormal," although many people confuse these. A sexologist will try to tell you what is sexually "normal," while a theologist will try to tell you what is morally "right." The sexologist and the theologist might not always agree. Sexologists loudly and unanimously proclaim that both cunnilingus and fellatio are perfectly normal (before, after, or instead of genital intercourse)!

If men had been born with penises on their chins, they would probably eat and screw at the same time - and that would be normal also. This concept is by no means an original thought of mine. In the late Eighteenth century, chinstrap-dildos were made and sold in France. In this attempt to improve on nature, a dildo was held in place on the chin by means of one strap that went over the top of the man's head and another that went around the back of his neck. With this contraption, Frenchmen could indeed lick and penetrate simultaneously!

Fortunately, many old discoveries are re-discovered and, to my delight, I noted a new item in one of my favorite sex toy catalogs. Called "The Accommodator," this accessory is a modern day version of the Eighteenth centry invention! The catalog peaks our curiosity by describing this improvement on nature as follows:

This soft, supple latex chin dong straps over the head for extra stimulation and hands-free fun during cunnilingus. Measuring 3 1/2 to 1 1/2 " wide, this flesh-colored phallus fits securely onto the wearer's chin for penetrating pleasures she'll love! Slip it on and slip it in!

> **Resource Tip**
>
> *The Accommodator can be purchased at a very resonable price from* **Adam & Eve**, *P.O. Box 800, Carrboro, NC 27510.*

IS CUNNILINGUS IMMORAL?

Questions of "right" and "wrong," and of "good" and "bad" are questions of morality. A conservative skeptic might ask, "Is oral sex immoral?" Those who would argue for procreation, at the exclusion of recreation, might do so on moral grounds. The idea that sex is only for reproduction has a long history. Thomas Aquinas, in the Thirteenth century, argued persuasively (in his time) that God intended intercourse to end in a pregnancy. Making babies was good, but making fun was bad, particularly when precious sperm was "wasted" or "misused!" To seek such wasteful pleasures would demonstrate a "grave moral disorder." The folks today who believe that forbidden pleasures of the flesh are sinful, would certainly brand the "eating of a fur burger" as an immoral practice, if for no other reason than it feels so darn good!

This negative perception of oral sex persists, despite the total lack of clear biblical condemnation for lovingly placing one's mouth on the genitals of a willing partner. Even without a strong basis in either the **Old** or **New Testaments**, oral-genital contact has been thought to violate the Judeo-Christian code of morality. However, if one wishes to go strictly by written scripture, since there is nothing in the Bible that specifically prohibits oral sex, we must conclude that there is nothing inherently immoral about the act!

At the Council of Jamnia in 100 A.D., the Song of Songs, Solomon's voluptuous and erotic song of love, was accepted into the canon of the Holy Scriptures. Arguments over interpretation have raged and will continue to rage, but the more realistic (and perhaps more liberal) biblical scholars see the writings as clearly being a sensual hymn in praise of joyful carnal love.

In this exquisitely beautiful expression of the sensual love that Solomon felt for Abishag, the following is recorded (Song of Solomon 4:10-11):

How fair is thy love, my sister, my spouse!
How much better is thy love than wine
and the smell of thine ointments than all spices!
They lips, O my spouse, drop as the honeycomb:
honey and milk are under they tongue'
and the smell of thy garments
is like the smell of Lebanon.

The following is also found within the Songs of Songs:

My beloved is gone down into his garden,
to the bed of spices,
to feed in the gardens, and to gather lilies.
I am my beloved's, and my beloved is mine;
He feedeth among the lilies.

It would seem clear to most that in the first passage the male is praising the wonderful natural aromas of his loved one's body. He is intoxicated by her love and excited by her "ointments." In the second passage the female seems to liken her genitals to a "garden," down to which her lover has traveled to feed "among the lilies."

Physician Ed Wheat and his wife Gaye wrote a book entitled Intended for Pleasure, with the subtitle Sex Technique and Sexual Fulfillment in Christian Marriage. On page 83 of this book, described as "The definitive Christian sex manual," they write, "Anything is permissible as long as it is desired by both partners, affords mutual pleasure, and does not offend either partner." One would think that this would include consensual cunnilingus, which certainly provides pleasure for both the giver and receiver. However, by page 217 a different message is given. Here the authors portray cunnilingus as a "shortcut."

These authors write, "It is difficult for this couple to imagine that they are now shortchanging themselves, because they may both be consistently reaching sexual release, although without experiencing the unity and oneness that God has designed for their human bodies in basic sexual intercourse."

In 1977, a book entitled <u>Human Sexuality</u> was published, with a more precise indication of content being reflected in the subtitle, "New Directions in American Catholic Thought." The book jacket further informs us that this is "A study Commissioned by The Catholic Theological Society of America." In this book it is stated that "...critical biblical scholarship finds it impossible on the basis of the empirical data to approve or reject categorically any particular sexual act outside of its contextual circumstances and intentions." In another place it is stated that "While the <u>Bible</u> does not provide absolute dictates about special sexual practices, it declares that sexual intercourse is good, always to be seen, however, within the larger context of personhood and community." No specific mention of oral sex is made in this text, but again we see oral stimulation ignored and genital intercourse sanctioned and aggrandized.

It is interesting, however, that both religious and non-religious givers and receivers of oral pleasures are likely to describe their experience as "spiritual!" It is clear that rigid religious doctrine and very personal deep feelings of spirituality are not the same. Writers such as the Wheats have failed to identify the intimate bonding of "souls" and the union with nature that loving couples can share, not only through genital intercourse, but through the joyful exchange of oral caress.

Psychologist Dr. Victoria Lee has written a thoughtful book entitled <u>Soulful Sex</u>. in which she has attempted to demonstrate how spirituality and passionate sexuality can be integrated. Of note also is the book entitled <u>Lovers for Life</u>, written by Dr. Daniel Ellenberg and Judith Bell. These authors weave together issues of sexuality, emotional intimacy and spirituality, looking at our source of sexual shame and its impact on our relationship. Both these books go beyond religious dogma and proclaim the possibility of a sex life that is both passionate and spiritual.

Resource Tip

For a broader academic perspective on sexuality and religion, I would recommend reading Sex in the World's Religions (1980) by Geoffrey Parrinder. Of interest also should be The X-Rated Bible, by Ben Edward Akerley, Sex in the Bible, by Tom Horner, and Sex and the Bible, by Gerald Larue.

Despite the negative messages often concealed in the misquoting of scripture, many religious couples accept their consensual sexual expression and their unlimited sensual creativity as wonderful gifts, intended for mutual enjoyment. This is an echo of what Joan Ohanneson wrote in her book And They Felt No Shame. She writes, "...the challenge is to truly believe that our human bodies are gifts of God and signs of God's love for us."

IS CUNNILINGUS A TYPICAL ACT?

There is the question of normality and the question of morality, and it has been argued thus far that cunnilingus is both normal and moral. But is it typical? This is a different question. Behaviors can be normal and moral, but rarely practiced (atypical). So, among human beings, is oral stimulation a frequently practiced behavior? The answer is a resounding "Yes," although age influences the practice to some extent. Alfred Kinsey, in his book Sexual Behavior in the Human Female (1953) found that "...among those females who had had some, even though not extensive coital experience, some 20 percent in the younger generations had accepted such oral stimulation; and among those who had had more extensive coital experience, 46 per cent had accepted such contacts."

In a book entitled The Encyclopedia of Sexual Trivia, first printed in Great Britain in 1990, author Robin Smith cites an unknown study in the 1970s showing that oral sex occurred in 60 percent of marriages, and among married people age 25 and younger, 90 percent of them had experienced oral stimulation. Shere Hite, in her nationwide study on female sexuality published in 1976 as The Hite Report, found within the group she studied that 42 percent of these women orgasmed regularly during oral stimulation.

A survey out of England, published in 1994, entitled <u>Sexual Attitudes and Lifestyles</u>, found that 64 percent of the women studied had experienced cunnilingus as a regular aspect of their love-making, and an additional 5 percent experienced it less frequently. Almost 20 percent of the female respondents reported having received oral stimulation within the week they answered the questionnaire - probably identifiable in the group as those women with smiles on their faces!

In the most recent U.S. survey, entitled <u>Sex in America</u> (1994), it was found that 76 percent of the men between 18 and 44 reported that giving head to a woman was appealing. In a group of older men from 45 to 59 years of age, 55 percent reported that performing oral sex was attractive to them. Apparently, performing cunnilingus is more popular among younger men, born after about 1950 - probably the end result of growing up during the "sexual revolution" and the "women's movement." This was a freeing up period in our society, when sexual experimentation was in ("Make Love, Not War") and women were claiming their right to ask for what they want, both in society and in bed ("I am Woman, Hear Me Roar").

The same 1994 survey found that 68 percent of women between 18 and 44 found receiving oral sex appealing, but only 57 percent felt as positive about giving. Of the women between ages 45 and 59, 40 percent found receiving oral sex appealing, while within this same age group, only 31 percent were enthusiastic about giving head to a man. However, it is safe to say that the clear majority of men and women (especially between 18 and 44) find cunnilingus appealing and we can only conclude that Frenching a woman is a very typical behavior in most modern (liberal) societies.

Is cunnilingus legal?

We know that performing and receiving cunnilingus is normal, that it is not immoral, and that it appears to be fairly typical behavior among the younger portion of the US population. But is it legal? Behavior can be normal, moral and typical, but may not be legal. So what about the legality of licking a woman's genitals?

Back around 1500 B.C., in the Mesopotamia Region, the Hittites (one of the Semitic tribes) were under harsh restrictions when it came to eating each other. These poor folks lived with a strict law that specifically prohibited oral sex, even when the couple was married. That really was B.C. (**B**efore **C**unnilingus)! Suprisingly however, similar prohibitive laws remained on the books over the next 3500 years and, until fairly recent times, most states had laws against both heterosexual and homosexual oral sex. Such law made frequent mention of such things as "crimes against nature," "perversion," "moral deprivation," and "lewd and lascivious" conduct. Attention was called to alleged "sodomy and gross indecency," and the taking of "improper and unnatural liberties." Bernhardt Hurwood, in Joys of Oral Love (1975) writes "Most laws against sexual freedom are fantastically phrased, describing 'infamous crimes against nature with mankind or animals,' 'intolerable, unholy, monstrous acts against nature,' and so forth. It's interesting," he continues, "that the same lawmakers never felt required to describe [in similar terms] breaking and entering, murder or various other crimes where there is a definite perpetrator and a definite victim."

Resource Tip

For a fun overview of some of the legislative attempts to control our behavior, read Loony Sex Laws *by Robert Wayne Pelton.*

Amazingly, there are still states with these antiquated laws on their books - in fact, at last count, oral sex remains illegal in twenty-three states, the District of Columbia and our country's military services. The states where the law books still forbid oral-genital stimulation between consenting adults are Alabama, Arizona, Arkansas, Florida, Georgia, Idaho, Kansas, Louisiana, Maryland, Massachusetts, Minnesota, Mississippi, Missouri, Montana, Nevada, North Carolina, Oklahoma, Rhode Island, South Carolina, Tennessee, Texas, Utah, and Virginia. It is unlikely, however, that anyone would be convicted of performing or receiving oral sex if it is a private act between consenting adults, does not involve psychological coercion or physical intimidation, and no money for the "service" is exchanged. If these conditions are met, it seems safe to assume that oral sex is legal in most states, or not likely to be prosecuted in those states where it is not.

Kenneth Ray Stubbs, Ph.D., certified sexologist and certified masseur, reminds us in his book <u>The Clitoral Kiss</u> (1993) that "...oppressive, puritanical laws are contrary to the fundamental functioning of a free society." Dr. Stubbs sees the issue as one of freedom of choice and the oral caress as very much within our right to "life, liberty, and the pursuit of happiness."

But it probably is unnatural!

The anti-cunnilinguist might argue that oral sex, even though normal, moral, typical and legal is, after all, unnatural! To be unnatural, oral sex would not occur elsewhere in nature. But it does!! While the human female may be the only animal that can articulate a "Thank you," a wide range of domestic and wild animals engage in oral stimulation (often upon themselves). Given that humans are not the only creatures interested in nibbling and licking another's genitals, we must conclude that cunnilingus is a very natural act!

What about rimming?

The most obvious place to begin in our brief discussion of rimming is to acknowledge that anal licking is a normal human behavior, but a behavior that is far less popular than cunnilingus. Although atypical, it is certainly not unnatural. Anal interest occurs frequently in nature and we often observe other creatures sniff and/or lick the backdoor of another. Remember when your family dog shoved his nose up the dress of your Sunday school teacher to investigate the distinct fragrance of her derriere?

The reader should be advised that there are some health risks associated with oral-anal stimulation that are not associated with oral-genital contact. However, these can be greatly reduced by diligent washing, by keeping the licking superficial, and (for the really cautious) by using a latex or plastic wrap barrier. Remember also to compulsively avoid placing anything into a vagina that has been in the anus (unless it has been well washed between insertions). As with any sexual act, it is always safest to know your partner(s) and to trust that they are as concerned about personal hygiene and with staying safe as you.

Must be something new!

Someone might try to discredit the oral enthusiasts by describing the act as a hippie perversion of the 1970's, and as a spin off from the sexual revolution. "It is obvious" these oraphobics will claim, "that this perversion has grown out of the wild sex orgies and psychodelic hallucinations of that era's flower children." To the contrary, oral sex (both cunnilingus and fellatio) predates the "me generation" and the act was fully explored and enjoyed long before young people, wearing beads and tie-dyed shirts, sat stoned in coffee houses listening to the music of Peter, Paul and Mary. Oral sex has been described in writing, drawings and sculpture from some of the earliest days of recorded history. Furthermore, it's practice has been documented worldwide.

Judging by the tone of a book of "Studies in Sexology in Chinese Culture," entitled Sex in China (1991) by Fang Fu Ruan, the current communist regime is not very tolerant of sexual experimentation. It would be unlikely that a book on "eating a China doll" would be published in that country under the present repressive government. However, long before the communist came into power and beginning back around 200 B.C., scrolls appeared in China and Japan which, through erotic pictures, were intended to instruct couples in the fine art of sex.

Traditional Far Eastern religions at the time of these erotic scrolls taught that sexual union was the human counterpart to the cosmic creative process. The Oriental love manuals of that era, called "pillow books," portrayed sexuality as in tune with nature and seemed clearly to emphasize the practice of cunnilingus. The old Chinese religion and popular philosophy viewed women as sexually insatiable and inexhaustible. This belief system, on the other hand, held that male semen was of limited supply and, with each ejaculation, there was an irreplaceable reduction in the total amount of remaining seminal fluid. The strategy, therefore, was to satisfy the woman as efficiently and as frequently as possible, while conserving the limited male semen. Unlike the modern country, ancient China would have been a cunnophile's paradise!

By the Seventh century A.D., the Japanese were creating their own brand of how-to-do-it sex manuals, called "shunga," meaning "reclining pictures." While cunnilingus was clearly portrayed in these Japanese scrolls, tongue kissing is essentially absent. It seems that mouth and tongue kissing were, in that place and time, considered somewhat deviant and was allowed only at the very height of sexual passion. When kissing in the rose garden, it was more acceptable to kiss the lips of a woman's genitals than it was to kiss the lips of her mouth.

At the conclusion of a section entitled **A Guided Tour**, "a brief excursion to some of the more remote parts of the world to examine oral love," the 1975 editor of <u>Joys of Oral Love</u> concludes "What it all boils down to is that, despite widely differing opinions, taboos, customs and cultures, human beings all over the world have at one time or another to a greater or lesser degree indulged in oral practices ranging from oral-genital lovemaking to gentle fondling of the lips."

The appeal of oral sex has been with humankind in most every culture for a very very long time. This attraction to connect our mouth with our partner's genitals is a very powerful and primitive impulse, rising out of the sexual animal within us. At the same time, however, it is a glorious and profound celebration of our unique human spirit. Given the power and deeply imbedded source of this desire, oral caress is likely to be around for a very long time.

BRIEF HISTORY OF CUNNILINGUS

Westerners seem to have been slow in re-discovering oral sex and accepting it as a natural pleasure. We humans, the "naked apes," are blessed with very sensitive lips and tongues. Indeed, the whole interior of our mouths might be considered an erogenous zone. In Alfred Kinsey's Sexual Behavior in the Human Female (1953) it is noted that "It is not surprising that the two areas of the body that are most sensitive erotically, namely the mouth and the genitalia, should frequently be brought into direct contract." Given this natural responsiveness, the fascination with oral-genital stimulation probably has been with us since the dawn of civilization.

Oral sex was known to be practiced among the tribal societies of Oceania and a variety of positions appear in a three-dimensional portrayal in the erotic pottery of the Chimu and Mochia people. This unique and explicit pottery showing oral stimulation dates back to about 300 B.C.

Chinese and Japanese writings and graphic depictions of cunnilingus, beginning as far back as 200 BC, are mentioned in the section above. There is an old Japanese saying that translates as "When the cup is deep, plunge your tongue into it several times."

The old Far Eastern scrolls, and "pillow books," many of which have survived to present day, do not have the same enduring popularity as what is perhaps the most famous love manual, the Kama Sutra. This manuscript was written by Vatsyayana, a poet and philosopher who lived sometime between 100 and 400 AD. In India, when the Kama Sutra was written, no distinction was made between love and sex. "Making love" and "making sex" were synonymous. In the history of India, there has been an expression of disdain for oral sex, but a near obsessive need to describe it in great detail! It was not surprising, therefore, to find that in the Kama Sutra, "oral congress" was both praised and scorned. Instruction was given by Vatsyayana on ways for a woman to tease the "Lingam" (penis) of her male partner. However, Vatsyayana, by modern standards being something of a male chauvinist, placed less emphasis on giving oral pleasure to women.

It may well be that Vatsyayana was too worried about vaginal odors, as he wrote a chapter on "Things that take away the bad smell from the armpits and sexual parts of women." He is translated as advising, "If a woman wants this bad odor to disappear she must pound red myrrh, then sift if, and knead this powder with myrtle-water, and rub her sexual parts with this wash." As an alternative he suggests, "Another remedy is obtained by pounding lavender, and kneading it afterwards with musk-rose-water. Saturate a piece of woollen-stuff with it, and rub the vulva with the same until it is hot."

Out of the metaphysical Eastern writing of the Ninth century comes a manuscript knows as the <u>Chandamaharosana Tantra</u>. Within this mystical writing is the following instruction to a couple:

> She should have him suck her Lotus and show his pleasure. Inhaling the odor, he should enter with his tongue, searching for the Red and White secretions. Then she should say to him, "Eat my essence! Drink the Waters of Release! O Son, be a slave as well as a father and lover!"

Collections of primitive erotic art are much more likely to include portrayals of our playful ancestors engaged in fellatio, and it is only later that depictions of cunnilingus began to appear. The Tenth century stone carvings on the Chitragupta Temple in Khajuraho, India, and those from the same century on the Devi Jagadamba Temple (also in Khajuraho), for example, show many depictions of oral sex, known as "auparusgtaja," being performed on males. However, the Twelfth century stone carvings on the Rajarani Temple in Bhuvaneshvara, India, show many more portrayals of the "Yoni-kiss." The Yoni (woman's vulva) is highly honored in Tantric rituals and the Yoni-kiss is an erotic theme common in those cultures where mystical sexuality is celebrated.

By the Eighteenth century, paintings in India were appearing that indicate that in that time and culture mutual oral stimulation had not only become quite common but had been assigned special mystical significance. What we have learned to call the 69 position was, in Hindu texts, referred to as "The Crow." Within the same century in Japan, paintings of the 69 position were abundant. The Taoism philosophy of the time taught that mutual oral-genital stimulation created a special energy circuit that facilitated good health through the harmonizing of vital body elements.

Resource Tip

Those interested in studying the metaphysical philosophies of the East will find no better survey of this subject than that found in SEXUAL SECRETS: The Alchemy of Ecstasy. This book, said to be the product of more than a decade of research, has been described as the "definitive study" on sex and mysticism.

In such a short history we will cut quickly to more recent times for examples of oral passion in literature. John Cleland's classic erotic novel, Fanny Hill: The Memoirs of A Woman of Pleasure was written around 1750. Contained within this early pornographic work are many graphic descriptions of oral sex. In 1954, the Story of O was published in France. Author Pauline Reage includes several long passages on oral sex in this story, including the following,

> ...she moaned when the alien lips, which were
> pressing upon the mound of flesh whence the inner
> corolla emanates, suddenly inflamed her, left her
> to allow the hot tip of the tongue to inflame her
> even more; she moaned even more when the lips began
> again; she felt the hidden point harden and rise, that point caught
> in a long, sucking bite between
> teeth and lips, which did not let go, a long, soothing
> bite which made her gasp for breath.

Resource Tip

The serious student of the history of oral sex is referred to the excellent coverage in Joys of Oral Love *(1975), edited by Bernhardt J. Hurwood. A brief, but thorough, history of oral sex may be found in a chapter written by Maureen Duffy entitled "Attitudes to Oral Sex," contained in the* Encyclopedia of Love & Sex *(1972). For those more interested in first-hand experience, skip the books and begin developing your own history!*

ISN'T THIS STUFF PRETTY "DIRTY?"

There are those who talk about "dirty" books and "dirty" movies. They will go on to speak of the "filth" one finds in porn. At the same time when a child has stepped in a mud puddle we describe his or her "dirty" shoes, and when we walk past a pig pen we comment on its "filth." It is distressing that we use the same words for things that are sexual and also for things that are grimy. It is true that our bodies can get dirty if we play in the sand or dig in the soil. If we sweat at the same time we become both dirty and smelly. Luckily, a good hot shower with lots of soap and water will quickly remedy this rank condition. Since it is not uncommon for a person to describe their genitals as "dirty" and "smelly," the same solution is available - lots of soap and water. It is unfortunate, however, that many people (even after a thorough scrubbing) continue to think of their genitals in negative terms. If you think of your crotch as dirty, how could you ever invite your lover to bury his or her face between your thighs? If you imagine your genitals to be smelly, why would you ever want to open up your legs to be eaten?

We seem unable to shake off the remnants of a long history during which human beings lived without the luxury of soaps and deodorants, washing machines and air-conditioners - not to mention toilet paper. In the not too distant past, there were no hot water heaters, no dry cleaners, no laundry detergents, and no wash-and-wear fabrics. People's bodies and people's clothing must have become very dirty and disgustingly smelly! Back then, the stench of underarms and crotches could certainly have been overwhelming. Indeed, it is said that the French invented perfume not with the goal of simply smelling good, but in an attempt to conceal objectionable body odors! Even today the advertisements encourage men to spray deodorants under their arms and women to spray it between their legs! In the late 1960's, a large manufacturer of deodorants attempted to market a vaginal spray deodorant called, believe it or not, "Sprunt." The name selected was a poorly concealed combination of "spray" and "cunt." It was the same old message - natural body smells are unpleasant and the modern man or woman must do everything possible to cover up these disagreeable aromas.

A medieval physician is reported to have referred to a woman as a "temple built over a cesspool!" This concept is certainly not one that would stir one's appetite, but it is not hard to image how horrific the personal aromas of the Middle Ages must have been. The problem with the body odors associated with poor personal hygiene can still be found in many countries today. In the 1979 book by Dr. Mikhail Stern, entitled <u>Sex in the USSR</u>, it is noted that in Russia, "Poor hygiene is still widespread in rural areas." Dr. Stern states, "A peasant woman who came to see me was in the habit of bathing only twice a year: she and her husband lived in a hut on one side of a small partition, and their pigs lived on the other." Elsewhere in the book he tells of a patient he identifies simply as "R." This patient had had a strong sex drive but little knowledge of sexual variety "...until he came across a pornographic publication which informed him that it was possible for lovers to stimulate each other's genitals orally." The man apparently convinced his wife that she should allow him to go down on her, but "...the result was disastrous. Peter the Great had once instructed Russian courtesans to wash themselves thoroughly before receiving foreign visitors in their boudoirs. As R. discovered, the problem had survived the Seventeenth century. He was so disagreeably affected by the odor of his wife's vagina," Dr. Stern writes, "that he became impotent!"

Fortunately, in those countries that have adopted modern concepts of sanitation and personal hygiene, and with the aid of all the cleaning and sterilizing products now available, perpetually smelly bodies are a thing of the past. Regardless of a ton of dirt and a profusion of sweat, soap and water quickly freshens all the cracks and crevices of our bodies. Peter the Great was right in advising that you wash thoroughly before receiving a visitor into your boudoir.

Maurice Yaffe' and Elizabeth Fenwick write in <u>Sexual Happiness for Women</u> (1986) that "Perhaps the worst anxiety for a woman is that she will smell or taste bad to her partner..." They continue, "...provided your genitals are kept clean by daily bathing, they will have only the normal healthy odor of sexual arousal, which will be both pleasant and exciting for your partner." These authors advise that it is easy for a woman to check this by gathering a little of her own vaginal lubrication on a finger after bathing. By smelling or tasting it herself she can be reassured that it is in no way offensive.

The "liberated woman" shows no repulsion when kissed by a lover that has just come up from the "Y," their smiling face covered with the juicy product of her own passion. In the era of modern hygiene and modern medicine, it's time to end all the crude jokes about a woman's foul smell, and to celebrate the culinary uniqueness of her most private parts. If a woman's genitals and vagina are healthy and well washed, there is nothing dirty about these wonderful body parts that nature has tucked ever so neatly between her legs. Her natural tastes and aromas are addictive and unforgettable, and, contrary to popular mythology, only fish smell like fish!

THE MOUTH AS A PATHWAY TO THE HEART

Dr. Wardell Pomeroy, co-author of the renowned "Kinsey Report," has been quoted in the March 1975 issue of <u>Cosmopolitan</u> as saying that oral sex is "... an extremely intimate act of the most loving and giving kind." He goes on to say that "In many respects it is more intimate than 'regular' intercourse and provides the rewards that such deep intimacy can give." This concept of oral sex as a more caring and intimate act, even surpassing penile-vaginal intercourse (coitus), may come as a surprise to some.

Dr. Roger Libby, in his delightful glossary entitled <u>Sex from Aah to Zipper</u> (1993) gets serious when he states "...oral sex isn't something that should be taken lightly - it just should be taken and given as often as possible. This most intimate form of kissing is the most generous sexual gift lovers can give each other."

We have grown up in a most secretive and sexually repressive society that presents intercourse (in the dark with man on top) as the ultimate sexual act. Intercourse received this elevated status when it was narrowly viewed as having the sole purpose of making babies and was reserved exclusively for those joined in holy matrimony. Any other sexual expression was viewed as an "act against nature." Many couples, therefore, postponed intercourse until married, but in the meantime satisfied their libidos by doing everything else! With their noncoital play, there were fantastic (and even multiple) orgasms, the result of great variety and unbridled freedom with manual and oral stimulation. Intercourse had been so aggrandized in these couples' minds that they actually believed they were saving the best for marriage. For many people, "sex" does equal "intercourse," and such folks do not think they had actually engaged in "sex" unless there had been some serious balling (despite the many long hours spent fondling, licking, sucking and cumming).

Despite the aggrandizement of "coital union" as an act assumed to drive every woman to orgasmic ecstasy, we know that a lot of women are unable to climax with intercourse. All too often the much anticipated penile-vaginal event occurs, only to have the unfulfilled woman wonder, "Is that all there is?"

Resource Tip

Many women have discovered that they can increase the frequency of orgasm during intercourse by using the "coital alignment technique," or CAT position. A full description of this approach to intercourse may be found in the book by Edward Eichel entitled The Perfect Fit.

There is no reason why people cannot decide, for their own reasons, to postpone intercourse. Certainly abstinence from intercourse is a very effective method of birth control. Some may, for religious reasons, feel more comfortable delaying intercourse until married. It is important, however, that once intercourse is added to a couple's list of sexual options that they not discontinue all other sensual and erotic activity. Foreplay and afterplay remain important. It is unfortunate when a couple, that had discovered all the joys of intimate noncoital sex, forget everything playful and end up simply bumping their pelvises together. There is a lot more to sexual intimacy than just screwing!

SHAME, SHAME ON YOU

When I was a kid in grade school (back in the mid-40's), we would taunt a classmate if she innocently separated her legs and naively revealed her underwear. Catching a glimpse of a little girl's panties, we would chant in unison, "I see Paris, I see France, I see Sally's dirty pants!" The response was immediate - a tugging down of the dress, a bringing of the knees tightly together, a look of utter embarassment, and, most devastating of all, an inner feeling of shame. That hidden feeling of shame, although invisable, is terribly destructive. When it is sexual shame, it impacts our feelings of our personal worth as a physical being and our perception of the value of our genitals.

In our up-tight society, most of us have been ruthlessly taught to be ashamed of your sexuality. We grow up being taught that we must, with a real compulsion, diligently hide what must be quite disgusting - our genitals. Even on a topless beach a woman must at least wear a string bikini. A very small patch of cloth covering her genitals, with a string up the crack of her buns to hold it in place, meets the criterion. As long as she conforms to this rigid "cunt code" she will be "legal." If she keeps it covered she'll be OK. The guy on the beach, with his jewels well-packaged in a pouch, has equal immunity from the law. He must, however, keep his tool tucked! If either the man or the woman removes that small piece of fabric (the modern day fig leaf) and exposes what lies beneath, he or she may go directly to jail! We, in fact, call our genitals our "privates," although in our society it would be more appropriate to call them our "secrets."

Because of the body shame we have grown up with, we can publicly reveal almost every part of our body except what is "down there!" However, when we throw off the old shame and celebrate our sexuality, our genitals become very special. With these private parts so exceptional, so personal, it is only with a great leap of trust that we can allow another human being to not only see our "secrets," but to place their mouth on them. For most of us, our mother never told us that this oral stuff was acceptable. We never got permission from our teachers to do it, and certainly never heard an endorsement of the oral pleasures in our church or temple. So, when we say to another, "I want to eat you!" we are expressing a genuine and passionate desire that comes from a very deep place within our being. Never having been told that it was OK and never having been schooled on how to do it, we are not just acting out a ritual taught us by our elders. Rather, it is an instinctual request to celebrate the specialness of our partner's genitals and to offer something really exceptional for that partner's pleasure. In doing so, we also create the opportunity to experience our own special joy in that loving act of giving the oral caress.

It is easy to be lazy and careless when having intercourse. If you put your butts on auto-pilot and bang those pubic bones together, the act can be completed without a lot of fancy technique or emotional connection. A mediocre lay does not take much skill and a lot of people seem to be able to do it without any real sense of intimacy. It is different, however, to lovingly place your mouth on or around the most personal part of another's body and to eagerly taste their tastes and smell their smells. This is a total acceptance of, and affection for, that person's most hidden parts and sexual products. It is saying, "I want to know you totally and, in this time we have together and in this most intimate way, to share with you this spectacular erotic pleasure."

In reviewing my manuscript and re-checking resources, I discovered that Shere Hite, in her 1976 book The Hite Report, made the identical point. She states that "One reason women like cunnilingus so much was that they felt that for someone to want to put his or her mouth there was very meaningful. It implied a special kind of acceptance." She goes on to quote a woman who had written, "The fact that someone can love 'that' part of me means a lot."

THE EXPLORER'S MAP

Before heading into unknown territory, the thoughtful explorer consults a map. The neophyte traveler is encouraged to study the following pictures and to become acquainted with the topography of a woman's genitalia before venturing into this unfamiliar terrain.

As a woman lies on her back, the view up between her legs reveals, at the top, a mound of fatty tissue covering her pubic bone. This small pad of fat (covered with pubic hair) is call the **mons pubis** or the **mons veneris** (mound of Venus). This triangular area is also called the **pubis**, the **pub**, and the **mons**. The mons is, for most women, not particularly sensitive, although firm pressure on the lower portion (just above the clitoris) can indirectly stimulate the more erogenous areas below. Some women also like the teasing feeling they experience when their pubic hair is played with.

Betty Dodson, in her book <u>Liberating Masturbation</u>, observes that "The (Valentine) heart shape is not the shape of the heart in her chest - it's the shape of the woman's genitals when she opens her lips."

It is best to remember, however that no two women look alike, either between their eyes or down between their thighs! A woman's genitals are as unique to her as is the nose on her face. As with the variety in size of noses and penises, the length of women's clitoral shafts vary, as well as the size of their clitoral heads. The head of a clitoris is known formally as the **glans clitoris** and is by far the most sensitive part of most women's genitals (also called her **vulva**). The clitoral shaft, clitoral head, and clitoral hood are, in popular language, most often referred to collectively as the "clit."

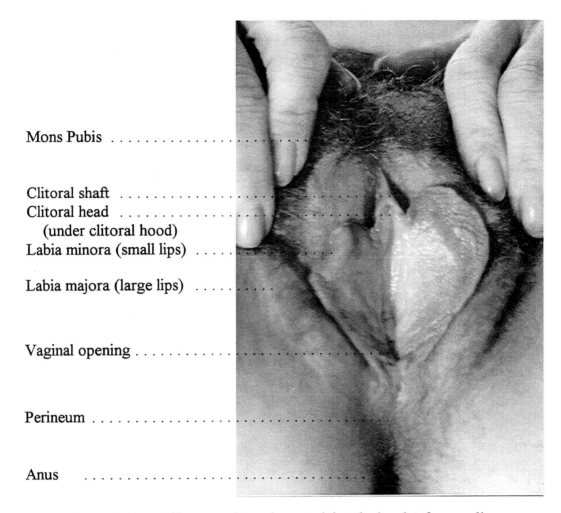

Mons Pubis . . . .

Clitoral shaft . . . .
Clitoral head . . . .
    (under clitoral hood)
Labia minora (small lips) . . . . .

Labia majora (large lips) . . . . .

Vaginal opening . . . .

Perineum . . . .

Anus . . . .

   In exploring differences, it can be noted that the heads of some clits
are completely covered by the clitoral hood (more formally the
prepuce), while other "joy buttons" barely peek out, and still others are
fully exposed. Some hoods are thick and puffy, others paper thin. Just
as the size of a penis is not related to the amount of pleasure it's owner
can feel, the size of a clitoris is unrelated to the pleasure a woman
experiences. Furthermore, a "hooded" clitoris is no more sensitive or
insensitive than one that is fully exposed.

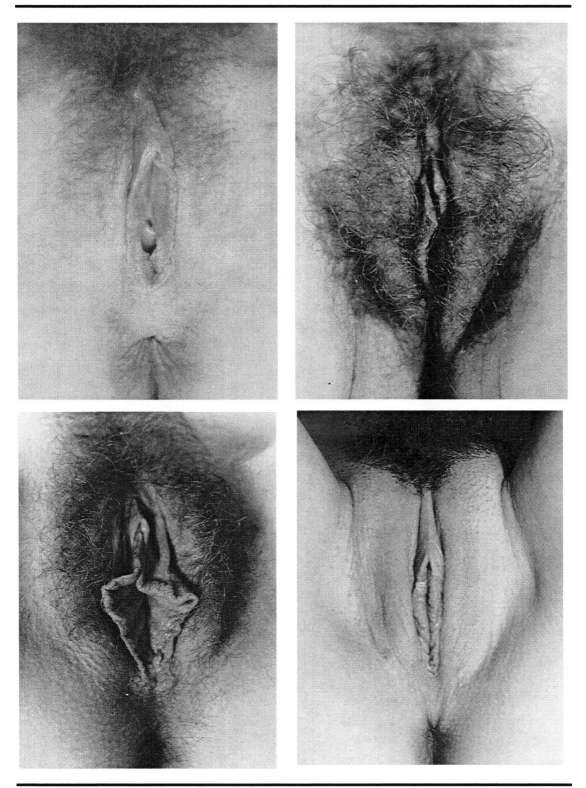

Not only does the length of clitorises vary, but the distance between the clitoral head and the vaginal opening differs among women. In some, this sensitive organ lies close to the opening, while with others the clitoral head is situated further from the vaginal entrance. There is no evidence to suggest that the closer the clitoral head is to the vaginal opening the more likely it is that the woman will orgasm during intercourse. Differences are neither good nor bad, but only mirror the many other physical differences we see among people.

The importance of the clitoris has probably been discovered, forgotten or suppressed and rediscovered many times over the course of human history. There have been periods in our history when it was not spoken of, and even today, mention of the clitoris as the source of female sexual pleasure is forbidden in many cultures. We do know that the anatomical artists of the late Renaissance saw and drew in great detail the clitoris and its related structures. The medical illustrator Casserio, in his book <u>Tabulae Anatomicae</u> (1627) clearly portrays the clitoris among the other details of the vulva. The illustrator who drew the cross-section of a woman's pelvis for the directions inserted in the box of one of today's best-selling tampon could learn much from Casserio. In showing where the tampon goes, the pubic bone, vagina and uterus are clearly portrayed, but there is not a clitoris in sight!

The clitoris has been described as being homologous (similar in origin and structure) to the penis. Both sexual organs are richly supplied by nerves and both become engorged with blood during arousal. In fact, in the not too distant past, reference was made to "clitoral erection." This description of an aroused clitoris has dropped from the literature, in part, I suspect, because it fostered the unrealistic expectation that this small female organ, in mimicking it's larger male counterpart, would enlarge significantly and rigidly point skyward. However, the clitoris of an aroused woman will indeed become engorged with blood, will increase in size and will firm up. Even though the female "hard on" is less dramatic (or at least less visible) than the male's, it is every bit as sensitive and certainly deserves very special attention.

The male penis serves three functions: It transports urine; it transports semen; and it provides pleasure to it's owner. While the penis "time shares," the clitoris specializes. The clitoris has but one function, and that is to provide pleasure! This small organ is indeed a woman's "joy button."

There is an old sexist saying that "Women are like boats - turn them upside down and they all look alike." However, the larger outer lips (labia majora) and the smaller inner lips (labia minora) of different women are quite different. "Turned upside down," women very much remain distinct individuals and within the many facets of their uniqueness is the marvelous design of these most personal possessions.

Resource Tip

Betty Dodson presents a visual portrait of a women's sexuality seminar in a video entitled SelfLoving. *Ten women, ages 28 to 60, join together in the discovery and celebration of their sexual pleasure. This video, which lovingly demonstrates the uniqueness of female genitals, is available from* **Focus International,** *the* **Sexuality Library,** *or* **Eve's Garden.**

With the same woman, her labia minora may change in structure and color as she ages or as she bears children. Also, a woman's labia might be uneven, with one side of her labia being longer than the lip on the other side. For some women the labia minora hang out from between the labia majora, and with others the smaller lips are tucked neatly within the labial folds. Exceptionally long labia minora have been called the "Hottentot Apron," a term which seems somehow pejorative. Size and length differences, as well as differences in coloration (even birth marks or moles within the vulva) are very normal and individual to each woman.

Betty Dodson, feminist author and sexuality educator, tells us in her book Liberating Masturbation (1974) that in looking at women's genitals she discovered that "The vaginal opening wasn't a hole at all, but rather pink-colored, soft little folds creating a different pattern in every woman." Again the uniqueness outweighs the similarities.

As the clitoris is by far the most sensitive of all the parts of a woman's vulva, it is usually clitoral stimulation that will bring her to the rapture of orgasm. For the majority of women who are comfortable receiving cunnilingus, being eaten by a skilled partner is the surest way to climax. A minority of women, however, will orgasm reliably during intercourse and some (a much smaller number) with "finger fucking." An even smaller number of women will orgasm with anal intercourse and a few with nipple stimulation. Responding intensely to nipple stimulation is known in quasi-scientific terms as "suctus stupratio."

A select group of very fortunate women seem to be able to orgasm solely with erotic fantasy. Yes, a few women have been reported by sexuality researcher Dr. Beverly Whipple to use their imagination alone to bring themselves to a full climax! This no-hands approach to cumming has become known as "thinking off." The point to remember from all of this is that there are a variety of pleasure spots among women, and you need, therefore, to completely understand your woman's unique anatomy, individualized sexual response pattern, and personal choices regarding stimulation. If you listen, you might be surprised (and excited) by the intriguing preferences some women have!

Women, for their part, are encouraged to take ownership of their own bodies and to become the expert on what works best for them! Psychotherapist and Sex Educator JoAnn Loulan, in her book <u>Lesbian Sex</u> (1984), reminds us that "Each woman likes to have her clitoris touched in a way special to her. Some like a slow, gentle, lingering touch. Others like a vigorous, active, intense touch. Some like to be rubbed back and forth; others up and down." Feminist Betty Dodson urges women to value their genitals and to become "cunt positive!" Especially in the early phase of a relationship, it may be risky for a woman to offer up the body she values without taking some control of what happens to it. A woman should not assume that a man (or even another woman) knows everything and she must, therefore, take some responsibility in teaching the partner what lights her fire.

It may be a myth that the first sexual encounter with a new partner is the best. It is true that there might be the intense excitement inherent in a novel encounter, but there might also be a lot of anxiety. Typically not much information is exchanged during the heat of the early sexual adventures. It takes time for some couples to become comfortable with the exchange of sexual feedback. It seems that it is easier to "do sex" than it is to "talk about it!" Effective communication is essential.

Verbal directions that change the focus of stimulation even a quarter of an inch can mean the difference between a fantastic orgasm and a sleepless night with an unresolved pelvic ache. Those who truly want to satisfy their women should forget all the "how-to" books and abandon the ego trip of trying to come across as a "sexpert" (sex expert). Forget all the preferences of previous women in your life and learn anew from your present partner. Find out what she has learned about her own uniqueness and closely follow her directions. If you give her the lead, she'll probably ask you back for more!

A WOMAN'S SEXUAL RESPONSE CYCLE

When a woman is not aroused, her vulva is dry. The large outer lips are closed and the clitoris and vaginal opening are tucked inside the fold. The vaginal opening is tight and the inner walls of the vagina are wrinkled and collapsed. Her cervix is resting down against the bottom vaginal wall.

Pheromones are the odorous secretions that, though subtle, are said to serve as powerful sexual signals between individuals. These pheromones are involved in the way a partner smells and tastes. With certain people, there is a very natural chemical connection, as our senses alert us to the possibility of a passionate encounter. A shiver up the spine as eyes meet or a sudden firming or moistening with the first touch might identify this sensory attraction.

While the pheromones, the "chemistry" a person feels for another, can move a woman to warm, it is usually the passionate kisses and tender caresses that turn up the heat. As a woman begins to get hot, her lubrication (referred to medically as her **transudate**) begins to seep from small pores surrounding the opening (or **introitus**) of her vagina. The exquisite aroma of a woman's lubrication, known also by the French word **cassollete**, contains chemicals that are even more arousing to men than are the pheromones. The aromatic love juices resulting from arousal must be brought up from around the vaginal opening to lubricate the clitoris (which does not lubricate itself).

With her arousal, the large lips being to enlarge and spread apart, revealing the clitoris and the vaginal opening. The head of the clitoris enlarges and, along with the clitoral shaft, firms up as it becomes engorged with blood. The entrance to the vagina opens and the inner walls of the vagina separate. The woman's uterus pulls slightly up into her body, causing the cervix to be elevated within the vagina (keeping it up out of the way during intercourse or other intravaginal play). The wet "love tunnel" has now smoothed itself out and has lengthened a bit in preparation for penetration. The vaginal walls are quite elastic and, as the old saying goes, can "stretch a mile without tearing an inch." A bit of an exaggeration, perhaps, but most woman's vaginas can stretch to accommodate most penises of a reasonable size.

As a woman escalates in her sexual excitement, her lubricating juices increase and her now sensitive clitoris pulls up under the clitoral hood (sometimes making it difficult to locate). As her passion mounts, she is likely to close her eyes and begin to concentrate on those exquisite feelings in and around her clitoris. When her body begins to reflexively tense her partner will know that she is on her way to having an orgasm. This **hypertonicity**, the natural tensing of her body, can last for a few minutes to well over a half hour. As this is the springboard into her orgasm, it would be unwise for you to assume that she will do better if she is relaxed! The woman on the edge of an orgasm, straining to get over the brink, typically does not appreciate a lover who stops stimulating, breaks her concentration and says, "Come on honey, you'll never cum if you don't relax!!"

As a woman hovers on the brink, she typically is quiet and may not want to be talked to. The words she enjoyed earlier may now be distracting as she concentrates on her breathing. She may exaggerate the tension in her pelvis, she may conjure up a favorite fantasy, she may focus all her attention on her physical sensations, or all of the above. Others will do none of the above and still get there easily! Each woman is different and will usually use whatever "triggers" they have discovered to have worked in the past. While unexpected novelty will sometimes spark an orgasm, most women do better with a familiar ritual that has previously proven reliable.

Resource Tip

There is a percent of women who have never experienced an orgasm. Years ago, Ms. Magazine sold a button that stated, "Don't die wondering!" Not wanting to be left out, countless women have found help in the book by Lonnie Barbach entitled For Yourself and/or Becoming Orgasmic by Julia Heiman and Joseph LoPiccolo.

When all is going well and the stimulation continues uninterrupted to the point of orgasm, the woman's pelvic floor muscles begin to contract rhythmically, with from six to twelve distinct contractions occurring. With each contraction there is a slight tightening around both the vaginal and the anal sphincters, as corresponding waves of pleasure sweep through the woman's body. Some women describe these as waves of warmth, while others use more dramatic terms alluding to pulsations, eruptions, explosions and electrical discharges. Sounds of pleasure typically emerge, with some women emitting a quiet series of gentle sighs, and with others crying out loudly in unmistakable screams of orgasmic ecstasy. Many women who discovered how to pleasure themselves at an early age, learned quickly that they would be scolded should they be caught playing with themselves. Therefore, at the point of these early orgasms they learned to stifle their sounds at the moment of climactic explosion. For some, it takes the unlearning of old inhibitions to begin to make sounds. While there is something to be said for a quiet celebration of pleasure, there is also something equally commendable about the "screamer" who does not worry about being heard by neighbors. I am clearly in support of those who let go and "make a joyful noise," regardless of the volume each woman selects.

Different women respond differently to clitoral stimulation during their orgasm. For some women, on-going stimulation intensifies the experience, while others find it distracting. One must learn quickly what his or her partner desires, as it would be a shame to get to this point and then ruin it! As the orgasmic contractions subside, the clitoris of most women becomes super sensitive. For some the moratorium on direct clitoral stimulation is brief, while for others it may be quite some time before stimulation can begin again. The multiply orgasmic woman is more likely to enjoy continuous stimulation right through each orgasm or, at least, the rests in between will be short. Be sure to ask! Since some women can take a licking and keep on ticking, learn how many orgasms your partner desires, and keep track!

After orgasms with oral, manual or vibrator stimulation, most heterosexual women (and some lesbian women) remain receptive (and at times eager) for vaginal penetration and, in fact, many women feel that the event is not over until that has been some internal vaginal stimulation by a penis, fingers or some other object with a similar shape. At the risk of reduancy, I will again remind you to learn about your partners' post-orgasm perferences.

Occasionally, as the vaginal canal opens during arousal and then contracts during orgasm (or as a woman moves to change position), air that has been drawn in is forcibly expelled. As the gentle blast of air ripples past the soft tissue surrounding the vaginal opening a vaginal fart can be heard. Playfully called "varts," these musical notes are cause for a shared chuckle.

Talking about what works in advance is strongly recommended. Communication during much of the erotic activity is also essential. However, when you rehash the event <u>after</u> it's over, trying to identify what your partner should have done, it is too late. If done carelessly in frustration, these after-the-fact discussions all too often come across as a critical critique, and feelings are likely to be hurt in the exchange of postmortem information. As one person said, "After sex, I don't want to listen to a book report!" On the other hand, with an erotic session of mutual and respectful reminiscence, information can be carefully exchanged that might prove useful in future encounters. Being careful and being constructive are keys to a successful postmortem review.

IN SWEET ANTICIPATION

If, in anticipation of an oral caress, a woman wishes to douche, it would probably be best to avoid using a medicinal-tasting product. Rinsing out with plain water should do no harm, would not effect natural flavors, and might provide reassurance to a finicky participant. Some women prefer the use of a mild mixture of vinegar and water, with very little risk of begin mistaken for an Italian salad! Most women need never worry about douching and most cunnophiles would never request it. In fact, it is important that a woman not over-douche with harsh chemicals, as the washing away of the vagina's natural fluids could actually promote irritation or infection.

A good washing of the external genitalia of both men and women is essential! Showering or bathing together adds to the fun of preparation and contributes to the sweet anticipation. Soap and water will do fine. However, if any degree of anal penetration is anticipated, an enema, followed by a shower, should be in order.

Remember the old wisdom - "Cleanliness is next to godliness!"

While perfumes may smell good, most have a terrible taste. Splashing oneself with fancy perfume, cologne, or aftershave could easily discourage the most enthusiastic licker. For similar reasons, foul-tasting lubricants, jellies or creams should be avoided during foreplay. Even the majority of the flavored commercial products are quite awful! However, some experimental folks have discovered the advantages of more natural products, such as honey or jam. The fact remains, though, that most connoisseurs prefer a woman's natural taste and unadulterated aroma!!

Just as you would not want to be poked and scratched with long or sharp fingernails (or a jagged hangnail), in preparation you should check your own fingers in anticipation of the oral and digital encounter. A clean mouth and fresh breath are also a requirement. However, gargling with a strong mouthwash just before going down on your partner could result in stinging or numbing the tender tissue of the person on the other end of your tingly tongue. Breath mints may make you kissing sweet, but may be unexpectedly harsh with delicate genital tissue. However, try experimenting. Some people actually like the tingly feeling of being licked or sucked just after the giver has swished with a minty solution.

It is always helpful to keep a container of warm water close by. It will come in handy for warming oils and lubricants, for warming non-electrical sex toys, and for any washing that becomes necessary. (Remember, if you wash the anal area, do not put the wash cloth back in water in which you are warming a silicone dildo!)

Vegetable oils, such as coconut oil, are wonderful (and inexpensive) massage oils. They are marvelous when warmed and applied lovingly in non-sexual caress. As one can not be certain about what is growing in these oils, you will want to avoid giving your partner a bladder or vaginal infection. I do not recommend, therefore, using these as a sexual lubricant on or in a woman's genitals. A man, being much less vulnerable to bladder infections, would typically enjoy having his penis oiled and stroked. There are blow jobs and there are also lube jobs!

> **Resource Tip**
>
> *I buy coconut oil by the jar in a natural food store and then transfer it to a re-cycled plastic squeeze bottle. As pure coconut oil has no smell, mix in a small bit of almond extract (that you can buy in a grocery store) to add a pleasing aroma.*

While most people enjoy being caressed with oils and have no allergic reaction, there are a few who have skin that is overly sensitive to some ointments. If you feel that there is reason for concern, test a new oil first. Before smearing the oil over the entire body of your partner, apply a bit on a small area of her skin a few days before performing your full-body massage.

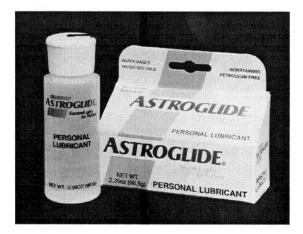

Sexual lubricants should be sterile water-soluble products, such as the much-used **K-Y Jelly**. The very slippery product known as **Astroglide** is frequently recommended by professional sex therapists. Never use **Vaseline** or other petroleum-based lubricants, which cause rapid deterioration of latex. Furthermore, a petroleum-based (and non-soluble) product might actually slow a woman's natural wetness by clogging the small pores through which her lubrication emerges.

> **Resource Tip**
>
> *K-Y Jelly can be found in most every pharmacy. Astroglide will be on the shelves of some drug stores, but may be more difficult to locate. It is worth the effort to write to the company to find the nearest source. Write to* **Bio-Film**, *3121 Scott Street, Vista, CA 92083.*

Couples using contraceptive foams, jellies, or creams need to be aware of the taste of the spermicide they are using. The early products were quite distasteful, but as manufacturers became aware that women loved oral sex as well as intercourse, some effort has been made to make the creams as tasteless as possible. It would probably be best, however, to insert the spermicidal creams after cunnilingus has occurred or to switch to condoms. Remember, however, that there are some suppositories that once inserted need time to melt. If you do not want to make babies, know the directions for proper use of the birth control method you and your partner employ. If intercourse is on the menu, keep all required contraceptive creams, gadgets and devices handy so as not to disrupt the romantic flow as you move from the appetizer of foreplay, through the main course of oral stimulation, and into a delightful coital desert.

Hair today, gone tomorrow

Some women may elect to trim long pubic hair and others may run a comb or fingers through their pubic hair to dislodge any loose strands that might otherwise end up lodged between the teeth of an eager cunnilinguist. Areas that have been shaved should be re-shaved, as stubble is rough on a tender tongue. Even if the woman does not have a totally "shaved beaver," but rather has what used to be called a "bathing suit shave" and more recently a "bikini wax," the area needs attention. If shaving is part of your foreplay, try using whipped cream instead of shaving cream, as any residue will be much more pleasing to the pallet.

If the woman is caught up in the sexual excitement when in need of a shave, she could put her hand over her pubic bone to protect the face of her licker. Guys also need to remember to shave before burying their faces between the tender thighs of their partners. A prickly face, covered with stubble, can be very distracting to a woman who is attempting to relax and focus on her pleasure. If duty calls but the man needs a shave, he can cup his chin in the palm of his hand to protect the woman designated to receive his cunnilingual favors.

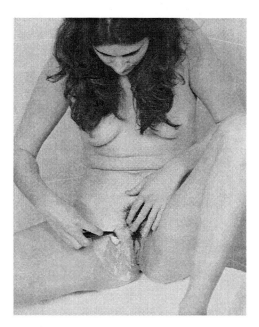

REMEMBER TO LOOK BEFORE YOU LICK

Looking at the body of a new partner is very exciting. Take your time in visually exploring every nook and cranny, every curve and crevice on her body. Look lovingly and lustfully to enjoy her physical topography, but also to critically inspect this new terrain. Look for sores, lesions, a discharge, or "creepy crawly" things. Remember, things like herpes lesions can appear around the waist, buttocks, and upper thighs; not just in the genital area.

Voyeuristic folks who need glasses for close up viewing will often need to make a tough decision - to see or not to see? If the eater enjoys the view and prefers, therefore, to wear glasses while performing cunnilingus, the receiver must be careful not to get carried away and clamp her legs tightly around the giver's ears! Picturing this crushing viselike grip of passion leads me to the awareness of at least one more good reason for wearing contacts.

SOME BABY STEPS FOR BEGINNERS

If you are hesitant about "going down" on a woman, but motivated and curious, there are some easy steps to lovingly sneaking up on a waiting crotch. If you have serious reservations, do not attempt in just one session to go from kissing her face to licking her genitals. Rather, plan as the first step to spend extra time French kissing your partner, being very aware of all the sensations in your lips and tongue. As you are deep kissing, caress your partner's wet genitals with the tip of a finger, stroking with the same rhythm as your tongue. If you are using the very tip of your tongue to touch the tip of your partner's tongue, use the very tip of your finger to touch the tip of her clitoris. If, in your partner's mouth, you are tonguing in circular movements, mimic the small circles with your finger around your partner's clitoris. In your mind, make a mental connection between what your teasing tongue and traveling finger are simultaneously doing. Experience the wetness of her mouth and associate it with the wetness of her vulva. Feel the warmth and softness of her tongue and mouth and, at the same time, experience the warmth and softness of her intriguing genitals. Taste the taste of her mouth and, correspondingly, imagine the sweet taste of her scrumptious vaginal fluids.

Spend time during this first session kissing and nibbling all over your partner's body, licking and sucking on her nipples in the process. Close your eyes and pretend that the nipple you are caressing with your tongue is her clitoris. On non-sexual spots on her body, taste her skin. Focus on that taste. Find non-sexual places where, when you sniff, you can sense her skin fragrance. Focus on that aroma.

Stay above her pubic hair during this first session, but bring up some of her vaginal fluid on a finger. Bring that finger close to your nose as you are sniffing non-sexual body aromas, for example, around the base of her neck. In your awareness, include these genital aromas with the other smells of her body. Place a small amount of her love juice near an area you have been licking and then include it, experiencing together both her sexual and non-sexual flavors.

This may be enough for your first baby step, but in between love-making sessions fantasize about the pleasures of cunnilingus. In the process, see if you can identify the source of any reluctance you might be feeling. Recall any negative childhood messages, but then remind yourself that as an adult you know there is nothing "dirty" about oral love. Imagine the sounds of pleasure that will emerge from your partner. In your "mind's eye," see the expression on her face as, in fantasy, you now begin caressing her clitoris with the tip of your tongue. Enjoy these visual and auditory images you conjure up mentally.

If, in reality, you are not quite ready for another step during the next encounter, re-do only the comfortable activities that you did the last time. It is important to remember that you should not push yourself (or your partner) into any activity that will increase anxiety. The purpose of the "baby steps" is to allow you (and your partner) an opportunity to relax and to progress slowly into a new expression of your sexual passion. With the gradual approach suggested, anxiety should eventually decrease and the beginner can then ease into an activity that had previously been off limits.

When you are ready to move on, extend your kissing and licking down below your partner's navel, but not onto her genitals. Kiss and lick around her sides and stomach, but (even though navels are novel) do not thrust your tongue into her belly-button unless you know for certain that she is comfortable with this probe. Some people are squeamish about their navels, so check it out first!! Move on down, nuzzling your face into her pubic hair while stroking between her genital lips with your fingers. Again bring up some of her juices to savor the aroma. Touch your tongue to the tip of a finger to again sample her flavor.

Having worked down almost to the good stuff, move to her feet and now begin to work up. Starting below her knee, kiss and lick up the inner part of one of her legs. Spend a considerable amount of time kissing and licking her inner thigh, moving up to the point that you feel her pubic hair brush against your face. Imagine yourself taking that final step. Imagine the smile of appreciation that will sweep across your partner's face. Imagine yourself exploring the three T's (temperature, texture, and taste) of each fold, ridge, and bump enclosed within the boundaries of her large outer lips. Allow yourself, in that positive erotic fantasy, to enjoy the oral pleasure you will simultaneously give and receive. In your mind, assure yourself of your ability to acquire even greater comfort with these new erotic behaviors.

Repeat each step as many times as needed to gain comfort and to fix a positive image of pleasure in your mind. When you are ready to move on to another baby step, repeat everything you have done up to this point. Now, however, run your tongue through your partner's pubic hair (assuming she has not shaved it off) and lightly brush over her labia majora with your mouth. Position yourself between her legs and kiss these large outer lips. As you kiss, sense her wetness and her fragrance, but without dipping in between her large labia. At this stage you may knock lightly at her outer door, but you need not go in (unless, of course, you are overwhelmed with passion and are suddenly fully ready to do some serious licking).

When ready for the next step, repeat all the previous baby steps, dwelling on those you particularly enjoyed. There is no hurry. It is important to think about the pleasure you get while orally exploring the wonderful fragrant body of your partner. While it is important to learn from her all the things that give her pleasure, when learning to be comfortable giving oral sex you should first focus on what turns you on. Learn all you can about the pleasure of giving pleasure.

When you get to the part where you are between her legs and have kissed her outer lips, place your mouth squarely on these outer lips, extend your tongue so that it enters the valley between her luscious labia. Lick upward with the tip of your tongue, feeling it traveling over the vaginal opening, over the area between the opening and her clitoris, and up onto and over the small firm bump (which is the clitoral head). If you did OK with that lap, start at the bottom and do another lingual sweep upward. If that went well, simply continue what you are doing! If you have come this far and are feeling comfortable, you are ready to strike out on your own. Be sure now, however, to check with your partner to discover what she likes.

DON'T HURRY HER HARRY!

A young woman confided that her boyfriend, Harry, always seemed to be in a hurry. He hurried through his meals, he hurried through his work, he hurried through his hobbies and he hurried through his sex! He approached this young woman as many men, remote in hand, approach a 100 channel TV. You've heard of these guys with the remote clutched tightly in hand - the notorious "channel surfers." Cut from the same cloth are the guys, like Harry, I call the "skin surfers." There's a brief kiss on the mouth, a light brush over a nipple, a hop-skip-and-a-jump across the belly, and a fleeting caress of the clit on the way down to the vaginal opening. (This approach reminds me of my approach to an after school job. As an impatient high school boy working in a service station in the 50's, I would prided myself on how quickly I could wipe the windshield, pop the hood, check the oil, and pump the gas!)

This persistent young woman eventually convinced Harry that she really enjoyed oral sex, and so, on his rush to intercourse he would pause briefly to grace her vulva with a few fleeting licks. Initially she was excited by his oral favors, but she again began to feel hurried. The message seemed to be, "Hurry up and get wet!" It was not long before she ceased being aroused by his tongue, as she was no longer even aware of his touch. She was too busy in her head telling herself that she had better hurry and get ready for Harry. As could be predicted, Harry eventually hurried himself right out of this young woman's bed, and, fortunately, she is now with a very patient lover who takes plenty of time to insure her total satisfaction. There is a valuable lesson to be learned here. Don't hurry her, or like Harry you will hurry yourself right out of your woman's life!

It is difficult for some, in the heat of passion, to slow down and savor the foreplay. Men need to remember, however, that for many women the foreplay (including oral caress) is every bit as important as intercourse - if not more so. When a woman has learned to appreciate receiving good oral stimulation, she is in no hurry to move on. Slow down! Take lots of time to appreciate the textures, the sounds, the aromas and the taste. Please don't hurry her.

FEATHERS, FUR, FANNIES, FANTASIES AND FUN

This may be a good sensual introduction with a new partner, as it offers a time to relax, to exchange quiet pleasures, and to talk erotically of an exciting agenda! This is a good opportunity, when the receiver is lying on her stomach, to lick behind her ears, the back of her neck, the small of her back, and the soft cheeks of her buns. Please remember when you are kissing around ears to kiss gently and quietly! A strong pucker and a loud "smack" can be irritating. A woman does not like feeling as though her ear drum is being sucked out of her head nor fearing that her ear drum will be shattered by an explosive sound.

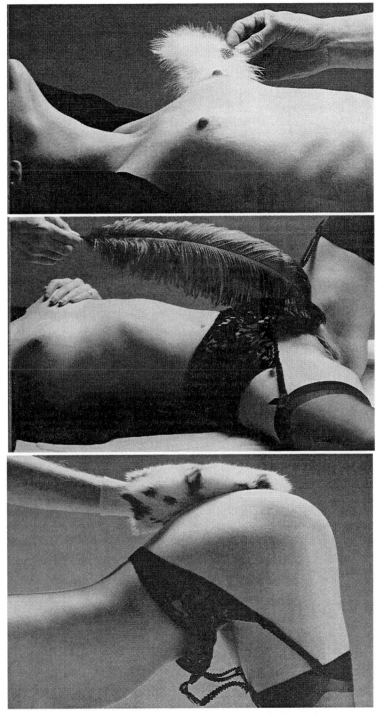

Women connect with words and sounds - vocalizations being at least as important as touch. To reach your partner through her auditory senses, fantasize out loud about sexual options, novel locations, and pleasurable experiences. Put into erotic words what you are seeing as you survey her physical landscape.

A fur mitt can add a sensual quality to your touch. Stroke your partner's body gently, focusing on those spots most sensitive to your furry caress.

As you "stroke" your partner verbally with your sounds, stroke her lightly with the soft edges of an ostrich feather. With her on her back, the sensual feather can be used to give pleasure on and around her breasts, her neck and ears, the inside of her elbows, and the inner surfaces of her thighs. Lightly brush her genitals with the tip of the feather - a gentle tickle might bring a smile to her face. After having traveled lightly over her body with the feather, go back again with licks and kisses to retrace an identical path. The wearing of sexy underwear or lingerie by your partner can add silky sensuality to this erotic play.

Resource Tip

*I like to order the two feet long hand-dyed ostrich feathers sold by **Good Vibrations**, 938 Howard St., Suite 101, San Francisco, CA 94103. You will have fun browsing their catalog of sexual toys and accessories. For sensual silk and satin, beautifully modeled, check out the catalog from **Frederick's of Hollywood**, P.O. Box 229, Hollywood, CA 90078.*

Take lots of time for your "finger skating," for the feather caress, and for the sensual giving of a thorough "tongue bath." Try not to miss any of her erogenous areas. With many women, however, there may be more skin surface that is sensitive than there is skin that is not! These women, when asked, "Where is your erogenous zone?" will reply, "It runs from the top of my head to the tip of my toes!"

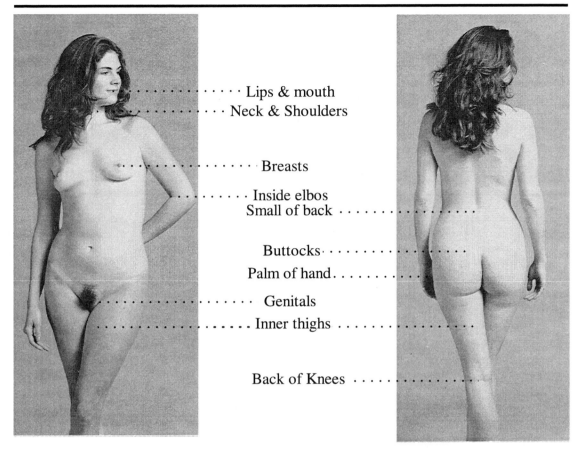

Lips & mouth
Neck & Shoulders

Breasts

Inside elbos
Small of back

Buttocks
Palm of hand

Genitals
Inner thighs

Back of Knees

The fascination with the erogenous zones of a woman's body is not new. During the Eighteenth century, for example, a miniature painting appeared in India, showing the erogenous spots on the female body. In that time it was believed that these spots changed each day during the lunar month.

This is a reminder that much of what we know today is not really new. We now take it pretty much for granted that many women experience touch differently, depending on where they are in their menstrual cycle (as well as the level of their arousal). It is because the responsiveness of these erogenous areas vary that communication during erotic and sexual play is so important.

Postpone diving between your partner's legs until you have lovingly connected between her ears with your gentle words and tender touch. Gershon Legman, in his book entitled <u>Oragenitalism: Oral Techniques in Genital Excitation</u> (1979) states wisely that "One does not begin caressing a woman with cunnilinctus. Often one ends there."

FINGER LICKING GOOD

As part of your foreplay, you might enjoy taking two of your partner's fingers into your mouth, saying something like "If you had a penis, this is how I would give you head," or (if more politically correct) "If your clit was this big, I would take the whole thing into my mouth and suck it like this!" Suck on these fingers, swishing and licking them in ways you would like your own genitals pleasured.

Lick the palm of your partner's hand as you would lick her vulva, making prolific promises of profound pleasures yet to come. If you curl in the sides of her hand, gently squeezing them together, the grove formed can be likened to the grove between her labia majora. Lick between these imaginary large outer lips, adding graphic verbal detail. "I love licking between the lips of your wet pussy!" Remember, of course, to never use words that are offensive to your partner.

Now gently spread two of her fingers and, with the tip of your tongue, symbolically caress the skin between them. Comment on your eagerness to spread her legs and lick what waits quietly at their moist juncture.

Within the 1995 movie <u>Don Juan DeMarco</u> there is an extremely sensual scene in which Don Juan, holding a woman's hand lightly in his, talks softly of women who ". . . have fingers with the same sensitivity as their legs." Then as he caresses her hand and lifts it close to his mouth he observes, "This fleshy part is the same as brushing your hands around their thighs and finally . . ." At this point he brings her knuckles to his lips and, one can guess, gently licks the tender skin between her fingers. She is his!

Spit & smegma

Use a lot of saliva when first licking around the clitoris. A good supply of spit will soften the mildly bitter taste of any remaining **smegma** under the clitoral hood that might have been missed when washing. Smegma, a naturally secreted oily fluid, will accumulate under the clitoral hood, just as it accumulates under the foreskin of an uncircumsized penis. A little special attention might be needed to wash it away. If some remains, however, though a wee bit harsher than vaginal juices, it does not have an unpleasant taste and is easily diluted with saliva and vaginal juices.

An ample supply of saliva can also be applied at the "back door" to dilute any residue around the anal sphincter (after plenty of hot water and soap have first been used). Saliva is a good (inexpensive) lubricant that is always available for facilitating either vaginal or anal penetration. As it is applied with the tongue, women typically love the application!

Lubrication, latex and lingual luxury

The safe approach to analingus is to lubricate the anal sphincter with a good lubricant and then to lick the area through a piece of latex (e.g., a dental dam or a nonlubricated condom that has been cut lengthwise and opened up). You might place a rolled-up dry condom directly over the lubricated anal sphincter and stick your tongue down into it. Kitchen plastic wrap could be used in a pinch, should intense passion strike spontaneously while standing in front of the oven and the preferred latex is unavailable.

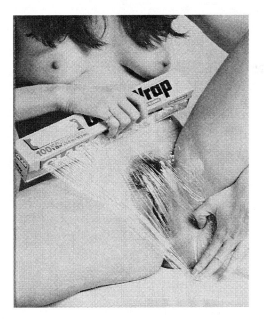

All but the most ardent analists would probably be more comfortable (and a lot safer) penetrating the anal sphincter if the area is covered with latex. Once more I will add the reminder to protect yourself when licking the vulva and/or anal area of women you do not know to be safe.

Resource Tip

Given the attractive novelty of anal stimulation, but the health risks involved, the serious analist should obtain and read the book by Dr. Jack Morin, entitled <u>Anal Pleasure & Health</u>.

EDIBLE WHEN PLUGGED

It is reported that in ancient Greek language there is actually a separate term to distinguish ordinary cunnilingus from muff diving during a woman's menstrual period. It is apparent that there were some Greeks in that earlier time that did not allow "the curse" to squelch their cunnilingual appetites. For the most part, however, we have been taught to avoid orally caressing a woman during her period. However, oral sex during any phase of a woman's menstrual cycle need not be restricted. After the first heavy day(s), a tampon in place allows for free oral exploration of the entire genital and, if you wish, anal areas. The only thing that may be missed is the abundant taste and ample wetness of the receiver's lubrication (most of which could be trapped inside the vagina by the tampon).

Nineteenth century author Aleister Crowley confronted a rigid Victorian taboo in his poem, entitled "Sleeping in Carthage," about cunnilingus with a menstruating woman.

> The month of thirst is ended, From the lips
> That hide their blushes in the golden wood
> A fervent fountain amorously slips,
> The dainty rivers of thy luscious blood;
> Red streams of sweet nepenthe that eclipse
> The milder nectar that the Gods hold good-

How my dry throat, held hard between thy hips.
Shall drain the moon-wrought flow of womanhood!
Divinest token of sterility, Strange barren fountain
    blushing from the womb,
Like to an echo of Augustan gloom
When all men drank this wine: it maddens me
With yearnings after new divinity,
Prize of thy draught, somewhere beyond the tomb.

Authors Beverly Whipple and Gina Ogden, in <u>Safe Encounters</u>, remind us of the importance of using a latex or plastic warp barrier when performing oral sex on a woman whose HIV status is unknown, especially during her menstrual period. Play safe!

A CHILLING PROPOSAL

For a novel sensation your partner might enjoy, try sucking on an ice cube just before licking her vulva. If your tongue is cold, be sure your heart remains warm. It is with mutual caring that couples find comfort in trying new things.

A WARM SOUTHERN BREEZE

To go from chilly to warm, place your open mouth low on your partner's pubic bone, covering her clitoris. Warm the area with your gentle breath, as you would warm your hands on a cold winter day. Back off then and blow lightly over her entire moist vulva - again, not a hurricane, but a soft gentle breeze.

Blow jobs are for him, not her

Never blow air forcefully into your partner's vagina, as there is a risk of creating an **air embolism**. While it is particularly true that forcing air into a pregnant woman's vagina could cause small air bubbles to enter her blood stream, this dangerous consequence could happen also with a woman just coming off her period. Since an air embolism might prove **fatal**, the best policy is to <u>never do it</u> with any woman at any time! This prohibition includes pumping whipped cream or other foams into your partner with an aerosol can!

Quarter moon

When your partner is lying flat on her stomach, there is only limited access to her genitals. However, this may feel like the safest position for a woman's first encounter, and gives you the opportunity to explore a lot of interesting skin with eyes, hands and mouth. Use feathers as suggested earlier, and don't forget the loving vocalization of words or joyful sounds. Kissing the back of her neck and shoulders is certainly suggested, as she stretches out prone before you.

Licking the small of her back has been mentioned before and is highly recommended. Kissing and kneading her buttocks is fun for both you and the receiver. Gentle nibbling on her buns adds novelty. Try licking the backs of the knees and then, with your tongue, work up the tender skin of her inner thighs. If it has not been previously discussed with your partner, this is an opportunity to explore her comfort with anal stimulation.

RIM AROUND THE ROSEY

In the quarter moon position, anal licking is easier to accomplish than is cunnilingus. With a willing partner lying on her stomach, the cheeks of her buttocks can be spread and the anal sphincter gently caressed - first with a finger and then with the tongue. The gourmet analist might do so at length, the sampler might do so only briefly, the cautious would do so with latex, and the squeamish would avoid the area all together!

HALF MOON

Greater access to your partner's genitals is gained when she supports herself on hands and knees. In this position, it is nice, while licking, to reach up under her body and experience the weight of her dangling breasts.

FULL MOON

Even with the half moon position, you would have to strain to lick the entire genital area. However, when the woman drops her upper body and, while on her elbows and knees, allows her hips to rotate up, good access to the area is given. The clitoral lick is down over the hooded shaft and over the partially covered head (as opposed to up under the hood and directly onto the head as is possible in other positions with the woman on her back).

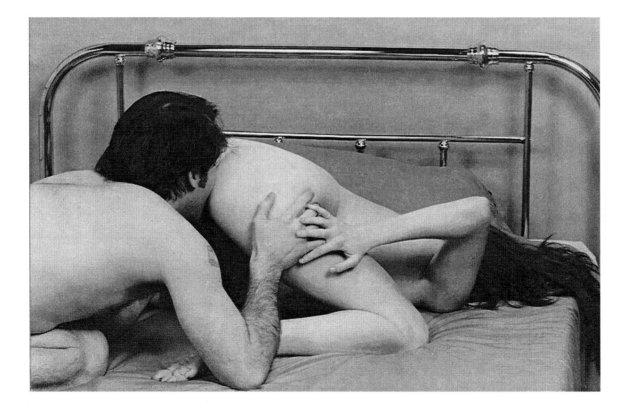

You could, I suppose, stick your tongue into your partner's vaginal opening, but in doing so in this position your nose would be poking into her anal sphincter. This gives a new erotic meaning to the term "brown nosing."

Don't come knocking at my back door!

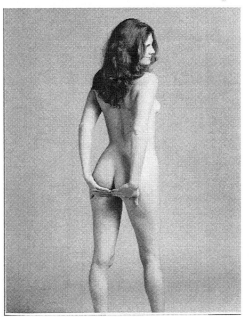

Remember, not every woman is comfortable receiving analingus or even finger caress of her anal sphincter. Your partner's comfort must be respected when it comes to these back door festivities. Know her limits and stay well within them. To pressure her may be offensive and a turn off - so be considerate!

THE "A" FRAME

The young and /or limber woman could spread her legs, bend at the waist and touch the floor. You, the eater, would then kneel behind her and come up between her thighs to enjoy her full assets. The longer the standing woman's legs, it would seem, the easier the access. The older or less limber woman can modify this position by bending over and placing her hands on a chair or the edge of a bed.

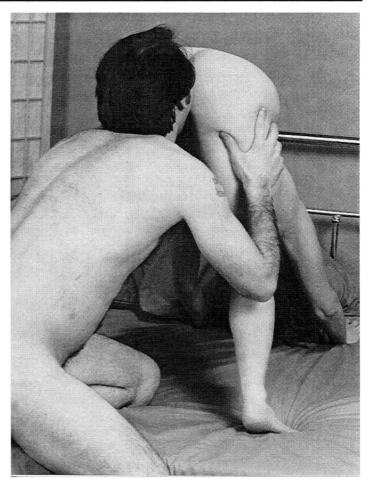

STAND UP FOR WHAT YOU WANT

Quite often, if you are undressing your partner while she is standing, you may naturally want to drop to your knees in front of her naked body. At other more passionate times a more expedient approach would be to go up under her skirt after panties have been hastily removed, or (if more frantic) up under the skirt with her panties pushed to one side.

In the woods or in the shower, where there is no place to lie down, your partner will enjoy standing for a brief oral caress. Although men who are receiving fellatio like to stand, with their giver on her knees in front of them ("kneeling at the alter"), a standing woman's clitoris (and all the rest of her pretty perineum) is tucked well between her legs. Perhaps if your partner stands with her legs far astride, rotating her hips forward, and you have a long tongue, some limited clitoral stimulation might be possible in this position. This can, however, be a real neck breaker for you! If she puts a foot up on a chair, however, there will be greater access. Regardless of the position, when the receiver is standing, it takes some craning of the neck to get to the goodies.

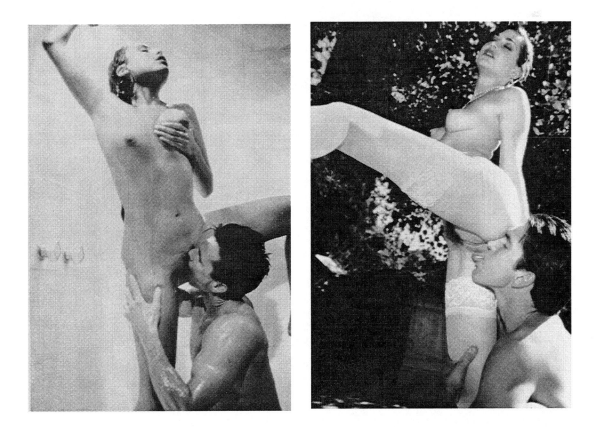

Admittedly, with the receiver towering over you, fantasies of dominance and submission can be entertained by one or both. It also allows an opportunity for you to reach up the front of the woman's body and experience her breasts from a different visual and tactile perspective. Additionally, being on your knees in front of a woman allows for an unrestricted embrace and caress of her buttocks. If you're into soft buns, this allows a wonderful opportunity to play.

If the woman is standing and you need to use your own arms for support, or your hands are otherwise engaged, it would be helpful for the receiver to reach down and use her own fingers to spread her vulvar lips. When it comes to gaining access to the right spot, cooperation pays.

SITTING THIS ONE OUT

Have your partner sit on a chair with her legs apart and draped over the chair arms or over your shoulders as you kneel in front of her. You will find that this works well (although your height might influence your comfort). Also with your partner sprawling on a couch, one leg on the floor, you have an opportunity to sit on the floor in front of her to eat. It may help if the woman extends her pelvis (and genitals) over the edge of the chair or couch. To save the fabric on your living room furniture, be sure to put a towel under her bottom. A good eating session will produce one hell-of-a wet spot, so be prepared.

TABLE THAT MOTION

There are many things that can be eaten on the kitchen table!! A woman atop a sturdy table can scoot her pelvis over the edge and, with legs wide apart, invite her partner to chow down. The eater may actually be able to sit on a chair during this erotic "box lunch." It would probably be rare that couples would plan to use a table, but if they did it would include, as a minimum, a pillow for the receiver's head.

It is more likely that a table would be pressed into service for a spontaneous encounter, when the need to express passion temporarily outweighs the need to be comfortable. Earlier the emergency use of kitchen plastic wrap was mentioned. If the menu includes some analingus, now might be the time.

An individual confined to a wheelchair might plan to use a table routinely or for some occasional novelty. Of course it might also be used for a spontaneous kitchen quickie. With the receiver on the table, the giver can wheel right up to this tempting tabletop treat.

Resource Tip

Individuals with a spinal cord injury that has impaired their sexual function will find the video <u>Sexuality Reborn</u> quite encouraging and informative. This video, funded by the Paralyzed Veterans of America, was produced as an educational tool by the **Kessler Institute for Rehabilitation.**

A TIME TO REFLECT

Many positions allow the receiver an opportunity to place a mirror in a spot that will allow a clear view of the action. The fun is doubled if you can find a position and an angle where both parties can watch what is happening.

It is for the same voyeuristic pleasures that a couple would strategically locate a video camera and videotape the visual and vocal details of their sexual adventures. Remember, with mirrors the scene only lasts as long as it lasts, but a videotape is forever. Mutual consent is required for the latter!

SIDE-BY-SIDE 69

In the traditional side-by-side "soixante-neuf" position, the couple lies on their sides, each facing the crotch of the other. The licking of the woman is down the shaft and over the clitoral hood - not under it. Licking around the vaginal opening may be difficult. With two women, the taller woman will have the advantage of being able to get her head further between the legs of her shorter partner. Given the availability and position of an erect penis, differences in height of a heterosexual couple seem less critical, except in extreme cases.

When orally caressing your partner's clitoris in this side-by-side position, you can insert your thumb into her vagina, with your hand then lying in the crease of her buns. As thumbs are stronger than other fingers, you can produce powerful internal rotations to accompany the external licking. You must of course find out from your partner if this adds to her pleasure or detracts from it.

Over-under 69

Couples do not need to lie on their sides to perform simultaneous oral sex. One person can lie on his or her back and the other can support him or herself on knees and elbows over top, facing in the opposite direction. In the over-under position, you will still be licking down over your partner's clitoral hood. If the woman is in the bottom position and is with a man, it seems to work best if her head is not supported by a pillow. Without head support, she will be less fearful of an unexpected "deep throat" maneuver, particularly if the man keeps his body raised a bit and allows the woman to move on him.

If the woman is on top, however, the person on the bottom may do better if his or her head is supported. The woman on top may lie with knees bent or more directly on the bottom partners' chest with her legs straight.

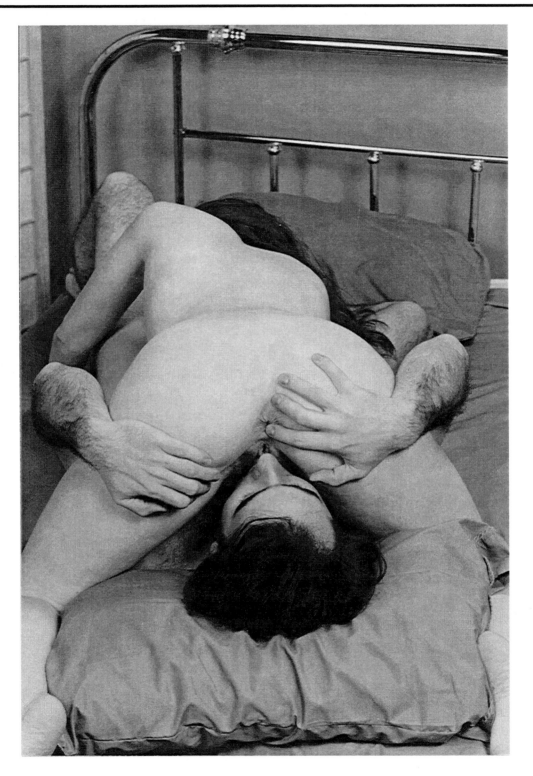

PEGGY'S PRETZEL

Peggy, being quite acrobatic, enjoys an unusual variation of the 69 with her female partner. The partner straddles Peggy's face, facing her feet, for receipt of her pleasure. At the same time, Peggy rolls her legs and hips up, presenting her goodies for her partner's loving consumption. Female anatomy allows for mutual pleasure in this upright 69 position, while a heterosexual couple may find it less rewarding. The Eighteenth century Hindu writings referred to this position as the "inverse crow."

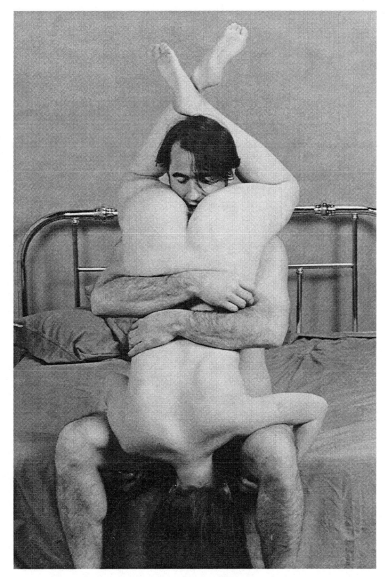

An alternative upright 69 is possible on the edge of a bed. More for novelty than stimulation, this approach to oral engagement is typically quite brief. With blood rushing to her head, the up-side-down partner will probably find it difficult to concentrate and will be quickly ready for a more confortable position!

SIT ON MY FACE, PLEASE

Your partner can sit on your face, facing in either direction. If she sits on your face facing your feet, she may need to bend forward so you can breath. Your tongue can probe the opening of her vagina and in licking her clitoris, the stroke will be down the shaft toward the clitoral head.

As licking up between the smaller inner lips, under the clitoral hood, and onto the clitoral head is typically more pleasurable, most women seem to prefer it when facing away from the eater's feet. When the woman stays in close she is essentially sitting on your chest.

If she leans forward and supports her weight on her knees, there tends to be more area accessible to your tongue and lips. It may help some women if, as the "sitter," she is kneeling in front of a chair and can rest her arms and head on the seat, or in bed, to use the headboard for support. This is a better position for licking up under the clitoral hood, and offers more freedom for a total vaginal, perineum and anal sweep.

Some women may feel detached from their partner while sitting on his face, as there is little of him that can be seen. A full length mirror, turned on it's side, might allow the sitter to observe the outstretched body of her eater. If the woman on top enjoys seeing her partner play with him or herself, the eater can self-pleasure while lapping the labia. The well-placed mirror adds to the eroticism of the oral encounter.

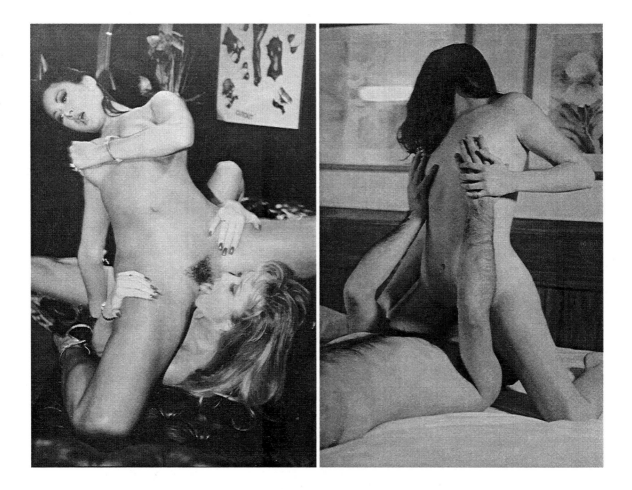

Many women become so absorbed in their own pleasure that they seem not to worry about being "serviced." At the risk of becoming repetitious, I will again remind you that there is pleasure in giving pleasure, and to be of service can be a joy.

THE POPULAR FRONTAL ATTACK

When your partner is on her back and is stretched out before you and you have come up between her legs, you probably have the best opportunity for upward stroking of her clitoris with your curled tongue. The advantage of a frontal attack (of the most playful sort) is the accessibility of the smaller inner labia and the clitoral area. Some vaginal probing with your tongue is possible, but it will not be deep and, at best, offers only a bit of novelty. For good vaginal and anal licking, the woman's hips must be lifted, supported by pillows or rolled up with her legs over your shoulders.

Up CLOSE AND PERSONAL

When coming up between a woman's legs in a frontal attack, the clitoris can be flicked lightly with the tip of your tongue. However, you can get up close and personal by pressing your mouth in tight, licking her clitoris with the flat surface of your tongue, and massaging her entire genital area with your open mouth. When up close and personal, do not forget to suck on her joy button. Some women even enjoy gentle biting of their clitoris and lips, but be sure to check this out with your partner before becoming too enthusiastic!

A LITTLE HELP FROM A FRIEND

Staying in the frontal position, with your tongue focusing on and around your partner's clitoris, take a reasonably-sized dildo out of the warm water (that has heated it to a more user-friendly temperature) and slowly insert it into her well-lubricated vagina. Remember, the woman must be aroused and wet before the insertion of this or any object. If she is feeling aroused, but needs additional artificial lubrication, use a water-soluble or water-based lubricant, such as K-Y Jelly or Astroglide.

Remember, the majority of commercially sold dildos are too big and too hard for most women. Avoid those made of plastic (often sold as vibrators) and use instead a softer one made of silicone.

> ### *Resource Tip*
>
> *No one makes and sells loving dildos like those available from **Eve's Garden**, 119 West 57th Street, Suite 420, New York, NY 10019. Before buying a dildo anywhere else, check out their catalog. Eve's Garden states "We grow pleasurable things for women," and they certainly have my endorsement.*

Ask if your partner likes gentle or vigorous dildo thrusting. Some dildos feel good when they are twisted, rather than pushed and pulled. All these magical movements can be executed right under your chin, as you continue to orally caress your partner's receptive clitoris. To be licked and deeply probed at the same time is, for many women, a fantastically exciting experience.

Take good care of your favorite sex toys (as they were probably expensive). Obviously you do not want to immerse a battery-operated or electric vibrator in water! Instead, wash these before and after use with a damp cloth and a little soap. If you want it to be as clean as possible, after washing it, wipe it with a mixture of alcohol and water. This is essential if you use the same toy with a variety of partners.

> ### *Resource Tip*
>
> *You could use a disinfecting cleanser called **Hibiclens**, available over-the-counter in must drugstores. There is also a product known as **For Play Adult Toy Cleanser**, which is sold by many of the establishments that market sex toys.*

Silicone dildos can be boiled in water for 5 minutes or, if you prefer, they can be washed in the top rack of your dishwasher. An alternative method would be to soak the toy for about 10 minute in a solution of one part bleach and 10 parts water.

Be sure batteries are fresh and, it the toy is electric, that you have a safe extension cord. Keep your toys handy so that the mood is not broken by having to go to another part of the house to retrieve your play things. Combining toys with oral loving doubles the pleasure and doubles the fun.

RAISING THE CURTAIN

Still in the frontal position and licking around your partner's clitoris, place the palm of your hand on her pubic bone - thumb and first finger coming down on either side of your mouth. With firm (but gentle) pressure upward you can slide the clitoral hood up the clitoral shaft. This will allow greater exposure of the sensitive head of her clitoris. At the same time, you can be holding her pubic hair up and out of the way. You can then spread your fingers and thumb to either side, stretching her outer lips outward, allowing greater surface area for broad sweeps of your tongue.

With your two hands, one on each side of your cheeks, use your fingers and thumbs to spread open the entire curtain of labia so you need not attempt to pry your tongue between the folds. In holding open the area, it is possible to make massive upward sweeps from the perineum, across the vaginal opening, up between the parted inner lips, over the glans clitoris, and on up the clitoral shaft. After an upward lick, do not bother trying to lick downward, but rather, upon arriving at the top move down immediately for another upward sweep. These long laps from bottom to top may be especially pleasing to your partner.

The advantage to an upward lick with labia spread is that your tongue can follow the grove and, using the inner lips as a guide, easily find your partner's clitoris. Remember, the head of the clitoris is located just at the point where the smaller inner lips join together at the top of your partner's vulva, and your tongue stroke will stimulate these tender labia as it moves up to her most sensitive pleasure spot.

Tease the clitoris with light flutters and then lap it firmly with the surface of your tongue. Raise the curtain and put on your best performance. Although you are the actor, your partner is the director. When on stage, follow her directions and you will be called back for many encores!.

A TASTY TWIST

With your partner flat on her back, and you coming up between her legs as in the frontal attack, have her rotate her hips a quarter turn. Extend one of your arms under her buttocks and up her back to help support her. This twist is great for licking sideways across her clitoral shaft, or making circles around the head of her clitoris. It is also good for perineal and anal sweeps, particularly if you lift her top leg to improve access.

FACE GRINDING

On their backs, with hips flat and knees bent, many women thrust, gyrate and grind. This almost reflexive movement may occur during stimulation and/or during her orgasm. It is important to know if the woman wants you to follow along with her or to stay in one place as she moves her genitals past your gracious tongue.

It is also possible to get a "bondage effect" if you wrap your arms under the woman's legs and around her hips. Hold on tight and enjoy the ride. This allows the receiver to move wildly and thrust powerfully without fear of "bucking you out of the saddle!"

Nipples and nookie

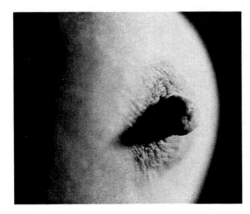

It is possible in the frontal attack position for you, the giver, to enjoy the view up over your partner's pubic bone and, while licking her clitoris, to reach up with one or both hands to caress breasts and nipples...making the "nookie/nipple connection." Be sure to use generous amounts of saliva and vaginal juices to lubricate the nipple and **areola** (dark area surrounding the nipple).

Roll her nipple gently between your thumb and forefinger, or trace slippery circles around the base of it. If the oral stimulation follows a sensual massage in which oil was used, the feeling of oily hands on soft breasts will be as pleasing to the giver as it is to the receiver. Those of you with "skin hunger" (a strong need to touch vast areas of nude skin) will enjoy this opportunity to look, eat and touch. In this activity there is something for everyone!

Going at it in the other direction may work just as well. That is, while licking and sucking on a nipple, manually caress her pulsating and well-lubricated clitoris. For many women, simultaneous nipple and clitoral stimulation combine in a mental package that is experienced as far greater than either stimulation alone. It is the principle that "the whole is greater than the sum of it's parts."

LICK THE CLIT AND TICKLE HER FANCY

With your partner lying on her back with hips flat and knees bent, while orally caressing her clitoris, bring your hand up under your chin. You can now, in addition to your licking, tickle her perineum, probe her vaginal opening and (if on limits) caress her anal sphincter. Available for your use is the abundance of your saliva and your partner's lubrication.

If your partner wants more fingers stimulating around her clitoris, she can reach down and add her own. Her fingers can now interplay with your tongue, creating a dance between your flicking tongue and her knowing fingers.

FINDING THE RIGHT SPOT

The frontal attack position is the best position for you to use one or two of your fingers for penetration of the vagina, providing stimulation of your partner's **G-Spot**. While licking up onto the clitoris, with your palm down insert one or two fingers (depending on her comfort) into your partner's vagina. Once penetration is made, turn your hand palm up.

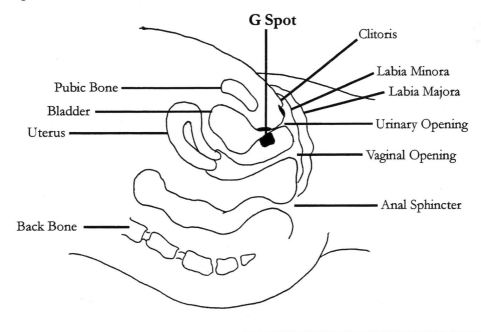

Begin rolling your fingers along the top surface of the inner vaginal wall, curling your finger(s) back behind her pubic bone and toward the inside of her vaginal opening. This is the same movement that you would make if you were motioning someone to "come here." Depend on your partner's reports to gauge the depth into her vagina and the degree of upward pressure she desires.

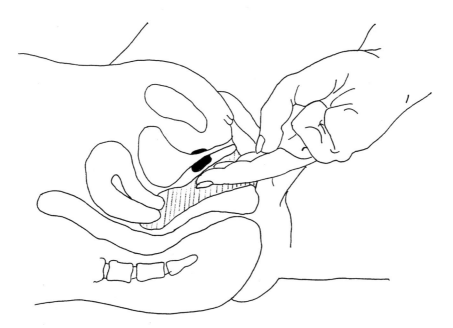

Diagrams courtesy of Dr. Beverly Whipple, Co-Author of **The G-Spot**

Resource Tip

To discover the excitement of reading the first book written on the topic, read <u>The G SPOT: and Other Recent Discoveries about Human Sexuality</u> *by Alice Ladis, Beverly Whipple and John Perry. Translated into 19 languages, this book is a classic.*

Remember, with or without G-Spot stimulation, some women expel a clear fluid through their urethral opening when they climax. No one has ever died from getting a mouthful of this "female ejaculate," so, if this occurs, ignore the spurting fluid and stay in touch with your partner's wet and explosive pleasure!

Resource Tip

House O' Chicks *produces and markets a wonderful variety of videos celebrating the beauty and uniqueness of female sexuality, including some showing women "ejaculating." Write to them at 2215R Market Street #813, San Francisco, CA 94114.*

BEST OF ALL WORLDS

Combine oral stimulation of the clitoris, lubricated stimulation of a nipple, thumb rotation in the vagina and index finger penetration into the anus. The insertion of a thumb and index finger into two openings has been called the "bowling ball hold." When a man eats, caresses, and penetrates as described above, the act has been called "the one-man band."

It has been reported that the withdrawal of a finger from the anus can produce a "pop," sounding very much like the sound when removing the cork from a champagne bottle. For some strange reason, French prostitutes of the Nineteenth century, performing what was called the "American corkscrew," would stand with legs apart and pop a finger or thumb out of their own anus! Apparently this is similar to the sound one makes running a finger along the inside of a cheek and "popping" it out of the mouth.

Remember that you should never ever take a finger or other object from a woman's anus and, without washing it, insert it into her vagina .

THE FLAT OUT LAIR

A flat out lair is not a woman who blatantly distorts the truth. Rather, it has been found that some women, on their backs, prefer keeping their legs and hips flat. For them, this allows an increase in pelvic muscle tension (hypertonicity), and serves as a trigger to facilitate an orgasm.

Other women prefer this position because the position of their legs protects a very sensitive clitoris from direct stimulation. Regardless of the woman's motive, this flat out position limits the cunnilinguist's creativity and access to the woman's vagina and perineum. However, your partner's preference should always prevail.

THE "T" FORMATION

Some women like receiving a very focused side-to-side licking (or flicking) of the clitoral shaft. This may be accomplished by the woman lying flat and the eater approaching from the side. In this position some expressiveness and creativity is lost, but it is possible to circle around the clitoris with your tongue (as well as perform the side-to-side stroke mentioned above). Remember, if it works for your partner, you may have to sacrifice novelty in the interest of providing the special pleasure of her choice.

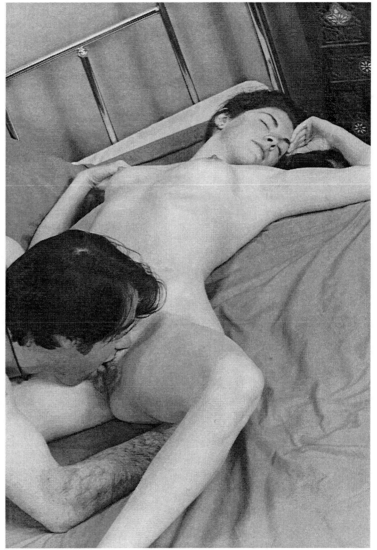

MINDY'S MISERY

Mindy tells of a position she likes, although she looks quite miserable when in it. Starting on her back she then brings her legs back toward her head. In this acrobatic maneuver, her hips are rolled up, allowing her partner to come up behind her on his (or her) knees. The giver now has a full range for licking and the receiver enjoys a good view of the action. The creative lover, in plain view and with a talented tongue, will quickly discover how to put his Mindy out of her misery!

GETTING INTO THE SWING OF IT

A review of an adult sex toy catalog reveals a variety of swings, slings, stirrups, and hammocks for suspending your loved one above the floor. Depending on the design of the contraption and the dexterity of your partner, a number of "spread eagle" positions are possible. A suspended "split beaver" becomes readily available to a kneeling cunnilinguist.

If interested, all you need is from $125.00 (for a web swing) up to $400.00 (for a more versatile leather sling). You must also be willing to screw one or more large eye hooks into your ceiling and/or walls! One "love swing" is advertised as follows:

Now you can be a REAL swinger! Hop on this sturdy "hot seat," put your legs through the stirrups and enjoy the ride....Suspends from overhead beams or doorways. Comes with all the hardware and instructions you need for full assembly and installation. Stainless steel with durable nylon web straps.

The ad for this lover's "hot seat" suggests that you could leave the swing in place for your next party. "Be daring and leave it up as a conversation piece!" I would not recommend , however, that you do so for a family gathering!

Resource Tip

*For information on one type of love swing, write **The Swing**, 1298 South Virginia, Reno, NV 89502. A more economical model can be found in an **Adam & Eve** catalog, P.O. Box 800, Carrboro, NC 27510, while the most expensive leather slings can be ordered from **Voyages**, P.O. Box 78550, San Francisco, CA 94107.*

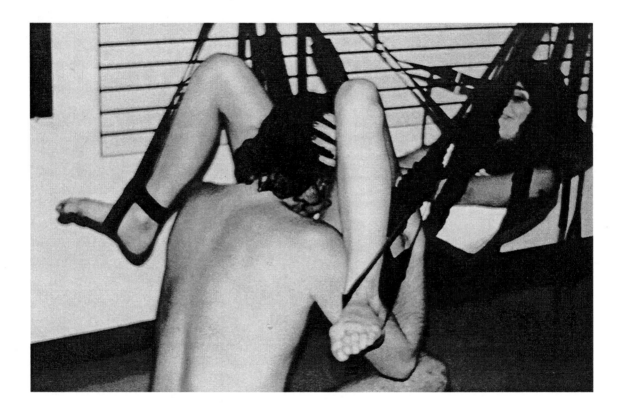

A creative shopper often finds less expensive alternatives which, although not specifically designed for the purpose you have in mind, still will work quite well. String and nylon twine hammocks can be found in many garden supply and yard accessory catalogs. If the design is right and the users are clever, what can be hung from a tree in your yard can be hung from a hook in your bedroom.

> **Resource Tip**
>
> The **Gardener's Supply Company** catalog offers a "hammock chair" of durable nylon twine for under $100.00. Check it out by writing to 128 Interval Road, Burlington, VT 05401 and requesting their catalog. Don't look for any sex toys in their listings, but if you like gardening, you'll enjoy their products. Voice of the Mountains catalog shows a wonderful hammock chair for under $200.00. Write to the **Vermont Country Store,** P.O. Box 3000, Manchester Center, VT 05255. They guarantee that their chair is "Cheaper than stress therapy." Enjoy their wide range of country-living products, but don't expect to find any vibrators listed. These good folks can provide the chair, but you will have to provide your own creative passion.

Novelty is important, but gimmicks and gadgets are never a replacement for consideration, respect, patience, and genuine passion! Be sure to exhaust all of your inexpensive creativity before imbedding stainless steel hooks in your ceiling!

THREE'S COMPANY

A threesome, or "ménage à trois," of consenting oral enthusiasts can be great fun! Frequently, one person at a time is allowed to selfishly receive the oral gifts of the other two. Turns are taken so no one need feel left out. Often the threesome is comprised of a heterosexual male and two bisexual women. With such an arrangement, the male is likely to break away to watch for a while - men being naturally more voyeuristic than women.

A ménage à trois can also be made up of two men and a woman, three lesbian or bisexual women or three homosexual or bisexual men. Come to think of it, why limit the number of players to three? Just remember to play safely!!

Double Tonguing

In a threesome, two givers can simultaneously lick a lucky woman's genitals. One of the cunnilinguists approaches from the side and over the top of the mons (pubic bone). This eater licks down onto and around this fortunate receiver's clitoris. The other eater comes in from the other side and under a leg, licking up into and around the vaginal opening. Now that's real pampering!!

Closing the Circle

In group sex (with three or more people), attention should be given to "closing the circle" so that all lucky participants can give and receive at the same time. A "daisy chain" of any number of individuals (of any and all persuasions) can circle around so all participants can simultaneously enjoy the shared oral experience.

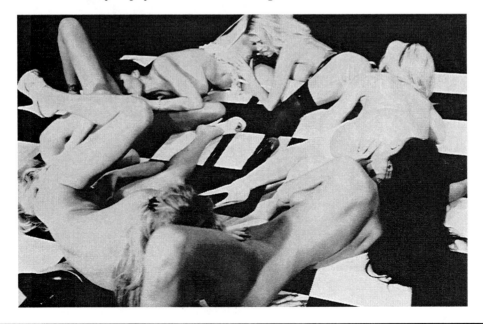

For the vast majority of people, active participation in a group orgy will forever remain a fantasy. If there is any consolation to never being asked to join a "group grope," it is that unlike real orgies, your fantasies are guaranteed to be completely safe!

MY TURN NOW

While simultaneously giving and receiving in the various 69 position can be much fun, there are some real advantages to taking turns. During your turn as the giver you can specialize in giving, enjoying a much greater range of movement, allowing an opportunity to find the best angle of approach. Being able to move around also allows you greater novelty, both in the direction of your lick and the direction of your look - that is, there is an increase in the visual scenes available to you for your voyeuristic enjoyment. As the giver, you are free to concentrate on each maneuver of your tongue, and to explore each vulvar nook and cranny with careful deliberation. Each delicious droplet of your partner's juices can be fully savored.

As the giver, your specializing in giving this gift of erotic pleasure allows the sensual signals received through your own fingertips to come into clearer focus. The temperatures and the textures of the woman's skin can be sensed. The warmth, softness. and smoothness of your partner's body will be more fully perceived.

When caught up in the joy of giving, the true cunnophile becomes selfish in demanding undisturbed concentration on this marvelous process of lovingly eating his woman. Both benefit - both the "selfish" giver and the "selfish" receiver! When it's your turn, you can take a break from giving and get into the specialty of receiving.

GIMME, GIMME, GIMME

When it comes to a woman receiving oral pleasure, a basic requirement is that the receiver allow herself to be selfish!! Well-known sex therapist Dr. Dagmar O'Connor playfully suggests women become "pigs" when it comes to enjoying sexual pleasure. With an eager beaver-eater between her legs, a woman must abandon all inhibitions, forgetting the negativity she had heard as a child. It is OK to quietly beg "gimme, gimme, gimme". With consenting adults, it is not better to give than to receive (although turn about is fair play). Lying back to allow unbridled passion to fill her body is the mark of a sexually-liberated woman. In being a "gimme girl," she not only reaches her greatest sexual potential, but she also allows her giver to experience the rich reward of giving unrestrained pleasure.

To TEASE OR NOT TO TEASE, THAT IS THE QUESTION

Many women love being orally teased. Provide some exquisite stimulation around your partner's clitoris and then, just as her excitement builds, execute a slow retreat to a less sensitive area. Allow the excitement to drop only slightly, then redirect your attention back to her more sensitive clitoral area. Again and again, as your partner's excitement builds to it's crescendo, slip teasingly away. Women who love to be teased report a more intense climax when the giver finally allows the orgasmic explosion to occur.

The student of cunnilingus is cautioned, however, that some women find teasing to be distracting at best, annoying at worst. Again the point is made that knowing what feels good and works best for your partner is essential!

WAKE ME WHEN YOU'RE FINISHED

Karie, a sensual college junior, expressed her love of being eaten and her greatest desire was to have a partner who would orally stimulate her for an extended period of time. It was true that she loved every minute of the long process of getting to her powerful orgasm, but it was also true that it took her quite a while to get there. Recently she found a male partner who seemed to enjoy having her lie back and be selfish. Initially he would lie down between her legs, bury his face in her crotch, and lick away until eventually she exploded in a tremendous (and very loud) climax. He continued to show this intense enthusiasm for the first dozen or so encounters, but then Karie began to notice that her lover seemed to be licking faster and harder in an apparent attempt to bring her to orgasm sooner. This was not to happen, however, as it had always taken her a while to cum, and feeling pressured certainly was not going to help. It was not long before she began to experience his stimulation as mechanical and to sense that he was getting bored. Not long after that he stopped eating her before she could orgasm, and not long after that she found herself a new lover!

Karie's story reminds us that some women need prolonged and concentrated stimulation to orgasm. It may be helpful if the woman signals her pleasure with sounds and movements. Sometimes loosening up both vocally and physically helps both partners to get into it. However, if moaning and grinding are not natural for the woman, assigning her the added responsibility (although entertaining to her lover) may actually slow her down.

It is really the responsibility of the giver to maintain his or her own enthusiasm. While eating, it helps to open your eyes and enjoy the marvelous erotic view. Each position offers its own visual and sensual perspective. "Humping" the receiver's leg or rubbing yourself on the mattress may help also. Furthermore, there is no rule against manually stroking your own genitals while busily tonguing a taco. This is an opportunity also to apply a condom (which you had conveniently placed close at hand). With the condom on, you can move smoothly from giving head to making penetration when your partner signals she is ready.

As the giver, make your own sounds as a reflection of the enjoyment you are feeling, and listen to yourself. Remember, sexual sounds can be a turn-on to both you and your partner. Maybe your partner, in her own rapture, will join you in that joyful duet of erotic moans.

DON'T FORGET THAT OTHER "ORAL SEX"

Talking about the wonderful sights, textures, tastes and aromas of your lover must be included in any oral sex adventure. Verbally, you can talk dirty about animal pleasures or, if preferred, speak delicately of a sensual spiritual moment. Non-verbally, it is great to moan with the pleasure of giving pleasure or to moan in harmony with the sounds of the appreciative receiver of your lingual gift.

Cats get a lot of touching because they instinctively purr. The more the sly cat purrs, the more touching she gets. There is something to be learned from a furry four-legged pussy!

GETTING THE JOB DONE LICKITY SPLIT!

Try lots of new things, adding whatever novel activities you and your partner enjoy. At some point, however, after much reading and an abundance of playful experimentation, forget the fancy stuff and get down to business. *There comes a time when it's time to cum!* When that time does come, do what you know works best for your eager partner! She'll be very appreciative of the gradual build up and most grateful for the much anticipated and fantastically explosive climax!

TO SPIT OR TO SWALLOW?

Given this heading, if this book had been about fellatio, this section would deal with the disposal of a mouthful of semen. With my interest in cunnilingus, however, I call your attention to another spit or swallow circumstance - the problem of an unwelcome pubic hair floating around in the eater's mouth. When the uninvited hair is loose, swallowing is not recommended! Typically it can be maneuvered out of your mouth without the receiver's awareness. Skillful tongue movements and a lot of saliva will usually do the trick, although playful fingers along side your mouth can then move the intrusive filament to a safe distance from the oral action.

When you sense that a wayward hair has become stuck between your teeth, there may be no way to dislodge it undetected. If the hair is still attached to your partner, it is not recommended that you pull away suddenly, as this will abruptly pluck the hair (root and all) from it's tender location. Rather, if the eater stays in close and continues as if the intruder was not there, it is likely to work it's way out, either from between the giver's teeth or from out of the receiver's mons. If it slips out from between the teeth, there is no harm done. If it is pulled from the receiver, having stayed in close will make the extraction much less perceptible.

The worst scenario is when the mischievous hair has made it's way to the back of your throat and is threatening to trigger the gag reflex! Subtle attempts to clear your throat may work, but when all else fails, it may be time to come up for air. A more concerted effort at retrieval can then be made. In this case, neither the giver nor the receiver should feel embarrassed. The area is not called "hair pie" without reason, and no one need feel distressed by a wandering strand. Take advantage of the short break in the action to laugh together about the temporary distraction.

AVOIDING THAT FALLOUT

As pubic hair seems, at times, to have a mind of it's own, falling out at will, it may help to run your fingers through the "patch" to dislodge any loose curly fellows before the eating frenzy begins. With a preliminary sweep, the risk of a spit or swallow dilemma can be significantly reduced.

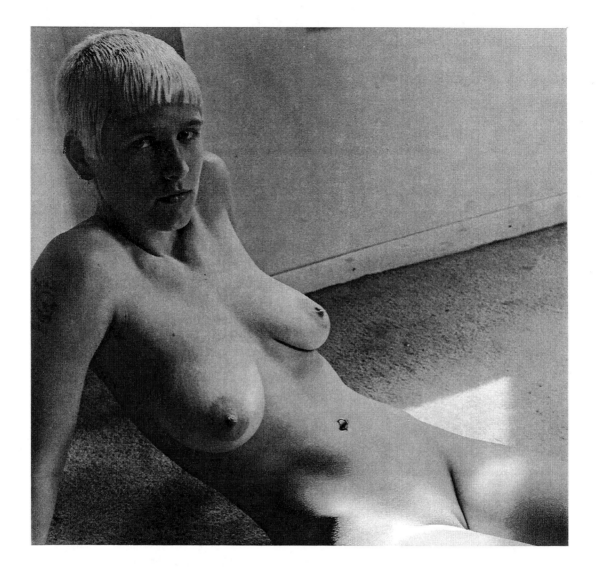

     Shaving the "pub" is, of course, another option. However, this may be more exciting and convenient for the eater than for the woman with the trimmed twat. A hairless crotch requires maintenance - frequent shaving and/or waxing. Stubble is irritating and a woman with a "five o'clock shadow" between her legs is likely to feel some discomfort of her own. Furthermore, the eater who recklessly dives into a stubbly crotch is likely to encounter a hostile prickly porcupine, rather than a friendly "shaved beaver!"

NEVER JUST EAT AND RUN

Fantastic cunnilingus happens in long-term relationships, but is also a possibility with someone you have just recently met. People who love oral sex don't necessarily wait until the relationship is well-established to initiate this favored (and flavored) activity. When a woman allows another person to place a head between her legs, to place a tongue on her most private parts, and to taste her most personal juices, she has given something of herself that is very very special. Because oral sex for many is a much more intimate act than intercourse, the giver should always thank the receiver for sharing so much of herself. This rule should be followed when the receiver is your wife of 30 years or an acquaintance of 30 minutes! If you're appreciative and express it, you're likely to be remembered. If you were also exceptional at what you gave, you will not only be remembered, but it is quite likely you will be asked to be come back for a repeat performance!

VARIETY OF LICKING STYLES

Before getting into a discussion of licking, I want to remind you not to forget sucking! Suck in the clitoral hood and clitoris itself (if it is large enough). Suck hard and suck gently - ask what you partner likes best. Suck in and gently "gum" the lush vulvar lips. Be careful with your teeth, although a very light and playful nip may be appreciated by some. The rare woman may even like a firm bite on her clitoris, but be sure this is desired before clamping down!

Licks, of course, can vary in firmness, from feather light to a very hard pressure. The very tip of your tongue, like a soft eraser of an artist's pencil, can be used to tease some tender tissue, or, like a house painter's brush, the flat surface of your tongue can lavishly lap a broad area!

The lick can be an upward stroking or flicking (as in lifting the clitoral hood to find the sensitive head of the clitoris), it can be side to side, or it can be circular. Your tongue can probe the vaginal opening in an unsuccessful attempt to thrust deeply ("tongue fucking" is a nice fantasy), or to gently "rim" the anal sphincter. You can also use your tongue to gently probe beneath the clitoral hood for a concentrated caress of the clitoral head....a playful pressing of her "joy button!"

Tongue flutters and flicks add novelty! The delicate eater might nibble, while the glutton will certainly devour. The oral maneuver can be slow and teasing or it can be fast and urgent. For a really different sensation, Dr. Kenneth Ray Stubbs recommends **hummin'**. In his book, The Clitoral Kiss, he writes, "Place your lips on or around any part of the body and hum". He playfully adds, "Make sure the tune fits the mood."

Never again consume an ice cream cone without appreciating the versatility of your tongue. Licking up into the cold treat with curled tongue is the same movement as licking up into your partner's genitals to lift the clitoral hood and caress the clitoral head. The flat-tongue approach to smoothing the ice cream around it's edges, catching the drips as they begin to run down the cone, is the same movement you would use in lovingly lapping a broad surface of your partner's vulva.

Practice, practice, practice!

Dr. Emily Sisler and Bertha Harris in the 1977 book entitled The Joy of Lesbian Sex, write,

> "The tongue is a muscular organ with muscle bundles
> extending longitudinally, laterally and vertically;
> like any muscle, it can tire. At the front it's attached
> to the floor of the mouth by the frenulum, which you can
> see and feel (and which, by the way, can be explored in
> tongue kisses). The frenulum varies in size, as do the
> width and length of tongues; muscle strength and
> susceptibility to the gag reflex vary too. All this means
> that, especially at first before practice makes more

perfect, extensive tonguing can leave your tongue muscles
taut and sore, and your tongue aching."

The tongue, like any out of shape muscle can become fatigued when used vigorously for an extended period of time. However, like any muscle it can be exercised and endurance can be increased. Extending the tongue out, repeatedly stretching it, is good, as is extending it and moving it from side to side. Curling the tongue for a series of repetitions should also be quite helpful.

As many cunnophiles have discovered, prolonged nookie nibbling may cause the jaw muscles to become sore also. Therefore, any exercise program should include repetitions of stretching the mouth wide open while thrusting the tongue outward.

GETTING A JUMP START

When young, we periodically experience a wave of sexual desire and with each experience of this emotional passion we are assured that, given the opportunity, we could easily become physically aroused. Desire, known traditionally as "libido," is the sexual appetite - the drive and the motivator that sends us off looking. If we have a responsive partner (or get lucky on a date), the excitement follows - men get hard and women get wet. To the young responsive man or woman, the sexual response seems perfectly natural. However, while *perfectly natural* sex is not *naturally perfect!* Unfortunately, people are not always perfectly matched when it comes to degree of desire.

Different people have different levels of this sexual hunger. Some folks are horny all the time, while others rarely think about sex. If two people are well matched in their levels of desire, there is rarely a problem. However, if one partner desires sex more often than the other, the discrepancy may become troublesome. It has been said that "If sex is good, it only makes up 20 percent of a relationship. However, if it's bad it can make up 80 percent!" Being out of step sexually has destroyed many otherwise adequate relationships.

Across the country, sex therapists' offices are full of couples who have always been or who have more recently fallen out of step. The largest category of sexual concerns centers around a **desire discrepancy**, with one of the partners frequently exclaiming, "Not tonight dear, I've got a headache!" If it is the woman who has the lower desire, she is likely to feel pressured and complain that "Every time he touches me he wants sex."

Contrary to popular belief, men also experience diminished sexual desire, and in such cases, it is his partner who feels physically neglected. When it is the man with the lower desire, he is likely to feel intimidated by the woman's stronger drive and complain that she is "over-sexed."

There are many reasons why men and women have low sexual desire or why at some time in their lives it has diminished. There are explanations also for why an individual might lose desire for a specific partner, while remaining horny in general.

Resource Tip

Whole books have been written to explore the various physical, hormonal and psychological reasons for problems of desire. One of the most recent and most academic is a book entitled The Sexual Desire Disorders by Dr. Helen Singer Kaplan. There is also a 1990 book written by Dr. Jennifer Knopf and Dr. Michael Seiler, entitled ISD: Inhibited Sexual Desire. The impact of certain medications and the effects of personal concerns and relationship problems are spelled out in detail in these texts. Dr.Janet Wolfe offers help in "renewing desire and intimacy" in her book entitled What to do when HE has a Headache.

While it is true that many of the problems are complex and may, in fact, have multiple causes, some of the problems of desire are more easily understood and certainly need not damage a relationship. Some people with low sexual desire have what has been called an "ignition problem." That is, their "starter" is broken, but their "motor" runs just fine. More specifically, since these people do not feel horny, they are reluctant to engage in sex because they can not anticipate their response. As one person asked, "Why get in the car if you're not sure it will run!" However, under the right circumstances it may be possible to "jump started" the motor.

Many people suffer from some form of the "I gotta" syndrome. "I gotta get hard!" "I gotta get wet!" "I gotta cum!" It is this pressure to perform and the subsequent fear of failure that causes a reluctance to start something when one is uncertain about how it will end. "I gotta make it work," is too often the silent thought when a eager partner approaches. In response there follows a quick inner survey of one's own sexual parts and a speedy internal search for ones own sexual feelings. If a tingle is not detected and a flicker of desire is not found, the next statement is likely to be "Not tonight dear, ..."

As stated, however, under the right circumstances it is possible to start from scratch in an attempt to jump start the sexual motor. The required ingredients are: trust, relaxation, and physical and emotional comfort. If the partner without spontaneous desire trusts the one with the stronger drive, is able to relax and not worry about performance, and is comfortable both in his or her head and in his or her bed, a jump start may be possible. The partner with the ignition problem should stretch out, relax, and be selfish in receiving the exquisite pleasure of being tenderly caressed in <u>nonsexual</u> ways.

With the receiver stretched out (and perhaps feeling a bit vulnerable) the giver must stay within certain guidelines. The person with the more demanding drive should begin the caress in nonsexual areas so that the receiver can begin to focus attention on "safe" physical sensations. The touch should be gentle and unhurried. The giver must be patient and non-demanding. It has become a popular saying among sex therapists that sensual touch should be **for play** and not immediately assumed to be **foreplay!** The giver should ask permission before moving from nonsexual to sexual areas and should follow any suggestions offered by the receiver.

Neither the giver nor the receiver should fixate on the goal of arousal! Remember, the initial touch is not foreplay. Rather, the strategy is to focus on the process, with the touch initially being for play. If it is a woman who needs the jump start, she should think, for example, "I like the feeling of having my nipple playfully licked," not "I hope this licking makes me lubricate!" The man, licking the nipple should think, "I like the feeling of my tongue circling this nipple," not "I hope this makes her wet!" To focus on the here-and-now feeling is to experience the process, as opposed to mentally rushing into the future in an attempt to accomplish a goal.

For many women who have broken starters, there is no arousal until there is direct clitoral stimulation. Kisses may no longer do it and breast stimulation, although still feeling good, may no longer be effective in stirring sexual excitement. But, if the woman is comfortable saying to her partner, "Here is my body, let's see what you can do with it," the very gradual approach described above, followed by a very loving oral caress of the clitoris can work wonders. With relaxation, a tender touch, and patience, the eventual licking of a dry vulva may create a spark that will make her damp and start her motor. Once her motor starts, you'll recognize it by that familiar road sign: "Slippery when wet!"

If problems of avoidance or low desire persist, couples should always seek professional assistance before the relationship is irreparably damaged. It is recommended that you check out the credentials of a professional before investing time and money, being sure that the person you will consult is qualified to evaluate and treat sexual concerns. Certification by the American Association of Sex Educators, Counselors and Therapists or by the American Academy of Clinical Sexologists is a good indicator of competence.

Resource Tip

*Rosters of qualified sex therapists practicing in your geographical area may be obtained by writing to the **American Association of Sex Educators, Counselors and Therapists,** P.O. Box 238, Mount Vernon, IA 52314 and/or to the **American Academy of Clinical Sexologists,** 1929 18th Street, N.W., Suite 1166, Washington, DC 20009.*

Fail-safe Sexuality

It is important for couples to adopt a "fail-safe" concept of sex - that is, a mutual focus on the joyful process and not on the final outcome. This will reduce the "fear of failure." In an intimate physical encounter, there is no room for a sense of failure. Since sex is not a competitive sport, scores should never be given and grades should never be assigned. Regardless of the outcome, the loving and intimate interaction should be considered a resounding success!

In case of emergency

It is known that even the most able young man may exceed his limit and push himself well beyond his ability to recuperate in time for a repeat performance. Now is not the time to feign a headache or to offer some lame excuse in a effort to salvage your reputation. Now is the time to demonstrate cunnilinqual expertise, and prove (to yourself and your partner) that giving is every bit as much fun as is receiving. Since many women feel selfish receiving and not being able to return the favor, playfully informing your partner that she "owes you one" may relieve her unwarranted sense of guilt.

We know regretably that age will surely take a toll on male potency and, as a man ages, he will become less and less reliable in his ability to "get it up" and "keep it up." There may, with the aging male, be instances when the passion between his ears does not travel down to the piston between his legs. This unfortunate happenstance should never discourage a sensual senior from "taking a whack at it." If he truly values

---

his partner's satisfaction and has a fail-safe concept of his love-making, he will, in case of an emergency, forget his own misfortune and pleasure his partner to completion with oral stimulation. If his partner enjoys simultaneous vaginal stimulation, finger or dildo penetration will be a welcome addition.

Resource Tip

*A lot of attention is paid to the sexuality of youth, with perfect bodies and limitless energy. Those wishing a resource on sexuality and aging should inquire about the newsletter entitled Sex over Forty, available from **DKT International**, P.O. Box 1600, Chapel Hill, NC 27515.*

One of the marvelous aspects of cunnilingus is that when all else fails, a good licking is still possible. In the midst of a thunder storm, when lightning has wiped out the local power station and a woman's electric vibrator has been rendered useless, the human tongue will still work. No assembly, no extension cords and no batteries are required for this versatile appendage. When a penis fails to rise to the occasion, either because of excessive use, illness or disability, or simply the consequence of aging, the tongue stands ready.

In an article entitled "The Dick Clinic," which appeared in the January 1996 issue of Playboy, author D. Keith Mano observes that the word "vagina" means "sheath" in Latin. He suggests, therefore, that we call the male member a "gladius," meaning "sword." I would observe, however, that "the tongue is truly mightier than the sword!" When the sword has failed, many of love's warriors have saved the day with an oral caress and satisfied their fair maiden fully through the expert use of an affectionate tongue.

So MANY STORIES, SO LITTLE TIME!

Fran's First and Foremost

Fran, happily married and the mother of two, was eager to share the story of her first experience. She wrote, "My introduction to cunnilingus was one of the most memorable experiences of my life, for it produced the first of many subsequent orgasms. The circumstances of this first orgasm are burned into my memory - not only because it was a first, but because it was so very erotic. I might add that I have become 'addicted' to oral sex, especially to receiving it.

It all started at the drive-in movie, where my boy friend (Steve) and I would go weekly. In the heat of the summer or the dead of winter, we were there to make-out (and supposedly to watch the movie). To tell the truth, I can not remember even one flick. We kissed and kissed for hours - through the first feature, through the intermission, and on through the second movie. The windows would get so steamed up from our heavy breathing and hot bodies that we never worried about anyone seeing in.

Steve and I were high school sweethearts and very much in love (as best teenagers can understand 'love'). For sure, we were sexually attracted to each other and both horny as hell! I still remember getting turned on just by the way he tasted and smelled. Looking back I realize how sexually naive we really were, but at the time we did not think so.

In the beginning of our relationship Steve told me that 'good girls' do not touch or allow themselves to be touched below the waist. My own urge to merge was so strong, however, that I could not buy his 'good girl' standard. However, I promised him I would abide by his restrictions. But, as you might suspect, as our relationship progressed our sexual experimentation did also. The time spent in the drive-ins (then known as 'passion pits' and 'finger bowls') pushed us beyond the boiling point. Despite Steve's initial reticence, we soon progressed to petting below the waist! Since I was the first girl he ever explored, he was surprised by my genitals. Following the initial caress, he later confessed, he visited a library to compare his observations with the clinical diagrams in an anatomy book!

We caught on fast to the pleasures of manual stimulation. With his guidance I soon learned how to give him a 'hand job' and even to be comfortable kissing and licking his organ. 'Doing him' orally became easy for me and I marveled at the tricks his peter performed. After all, this being the first penis I every played with, I had no basis of comparison. I was utterly fascinated! I especially loved it when he came. I don't know why, but it made me feel powerful.

Steve was willing to learn of my private parts, and professed to love the sweetness of my juices and the warmth and softness of my pussy. There was a problem, however. I could not entice him to eat me naked! The only way I could get him near my crotch was to keep my panties on! He would touch under them, but not lick my genitals directly. Since he would lick and kiss me through my panties I accepted the challenge. Being a smart lass (and maybe a smart ass), I began to incorporate a variety of kinds of panties into our passion pit sessions. My wardrobe of underwear ballooned! My goal on date night was to wear the flimsiest panties with the thinnest fabric I could find.

One memorable summer evening, we were both especially turned on as we made-out in our 'motel on wheels.' Oblivious to the movie showing on the screen, I became exquisitely responsive as he touched, licked and kissed me all over my body. I remember especially the gentle prodding of his fingers through my sheer panties, now soaked with the product of my sky-rocketing excitement. I ended up spread across the back seat, wearing only my skimpy underwear. Steve teasingly moved down my body with his mouth. Without touching him, I knew he had become hard as a rock. When he finally reached my crotch and began kissing me through my panties, I started to squirm and moan in response to the touch of his lips and tongue. I think my obvious response propelled him into more intense action. To my delight, he suddenly pulled down my panties and impulsively buried his face into my bare, wet and throbbing flesh. All I remember from that point on was feeling the softness of his tongue on my clitoris and, out of the blue, seeing stars! In the middle of a nameless movie, I had experienced my very first mind-blowing orgasm! After a period of recovery and a return to reality, we realized what had happened. Despite our mutual happiness, Steve solemnly vowed he would 'never do that again!'

It will come as no surprise that his promise was broken the very next weekend at the drive-in. From then on, all barriers (including lace panties) were removed and most subsequent dates consisted of eating (not at the concession stand) our way through double features. That is how, with my sensual high school sweetheart, I learned to love receiving oral sex. I'll never forget my first and foremost experience.. "

Sharon's Surprise

Sharon, now 40 years young, writes, "I became sexually active at a very early age, having discovered the joys of masturbation by about 8 and the thrill of orgasm by 10! As a virgin, I masturbated frequently, joyfully and without guilt up until my freshman year of high school. My self-pleasuring was accompanied with fanciful daydreams of love and romance. In fantasy, I was the queen of the prom and the football captain was devoted to the total fulfillment of my youthful passion. As I came in reality, in my fantasy the gorgeous young man of my dreams had just penetrated my wet and trembling body. In my mind, penetration became the trigger to orgasm.

My first lover was not the football captain and, in fact, never made the team. I had known Roger for years, but had never thought of him as other than a casual acquaintance. He was cute enough, but too quiet for me. A big party, a bit too much beer, and some heavy petting changed all that! I can not tell to this day if it was the beer or if it was Roger, but I turned on with him like I had never turned on before. We kissed, we groped, and we flopped around trying awkwardly to undo each other's clothing. I do not recall the actual sequence, but all of a sudden it seems I was on my back, legs in the air and Roger was probing around in search of my unexplored opening. The next thing I know I was feeling some discomfort around the entrance to my vagina and Roger was moaning like the top of his head was coming off! I became aware that night that penetration was not going to be the key to my orgasm, although it sure worked well for Roger! I was envious of the ease with which he came, but I persuaded myself that I would surely make it next time.

Roger and I did the 'dirty deed' six more times and, looking back, I now realize how lucky I was not to have become pregnant. Each time was the same - some hot kissing and then a rush into unprotected intercourse. Roger continued to ejaculate within seconds. By the last time with Roger it no longer hurt - in fact, I no longer felt much of anything once he entered me!

During my time with Roger I continued to masturbate and to imagine that the next experience of intercourse would provide the magic that would push me into the best orgasm I could ever have. However, each time with Roger our impulsive endeavors only resulted in my frustration. I never told him I was not cumming, nor of my need to satisfy myself at home.

After about two months, Roger and I broke up - not for sexual reasons, but because we just seemed to fight all the time over silly things. After Roger and during a brief dating dry spell I am sure I doubled my masturbation - deep in the familiar fantasy of the perfect fuck. I was sure it was out there waiting for me!

It was not long before Bill wandered into my life, cute as could be, but an unreliable 17 year old with more animal hormones than human consideration. Making a date with Bill meant nothing to him. I was stood up more times than the pins in a bowling alley, but, having lost my virginity with Roger, I was determined to have intercourse with Bill. Therefore, the times we were together were usually spent screwing our brains out in the back seat of his father's station wagon. Bill seemed to last a lot longer than Roger, and, for a while, I thought this was what it would take. At times we screwed until I was sore, but I was still unable to cum. As a result, I went back to my old practice of finishing myself off at home. Neither Roger nor Bill were exceptionally large, and so I began to fantasize about being with a guy with a big dick. Surely, I though, I would cum with a really big one inside!

Before I finally graduated from high school I probably went through three more guys and got to experience dicks covering a wide range of length and thickness. I still had no orgasms, other than those I would give myself at home. During the first quarter of my freshman year of college, I began dating Brent - a junior studying criminology and a desire to work within the prison system. Brent was well built and masculine, but amazingly gentle and romantic. I'll never forget his kisses and vividly recall my excitement when, on our first encounter in bed, he began kissing and licking my breasts. Even more memorable is the bewilderment I felt as he began kissing and licking my stomach, my inner thighs and around my pubic hair. I remember two simultaneous (but conflicting) thoughts - I was scared to death that he might lick my pussy and excited as hell by the thought that he would! Part of me wanted to pull him up by the hair and another part of me wanted to push his head down between my legs.

Brent did not leave the decision to me. He knew what he wanted, where he was going, and what he was going to do once he got there! With the first touch of his tongue I knew I was in for something different. What I did not suspect, however, was that I would explode with not one, but two orgasms in quick succession! I was exhausted and drained by the intensity of my cumming, but most of all I was surprised! Above all others, I will remember Brent - for his kindness and for his love of eating pussy. He was my teacher, and with him I learned to enjoy not only giving head, but that it was alright for me to lie back and be selfish. Ever since I have loved being eaten and, to this day, this remains the only way I can cum with a partner. I do not see this as a disability, for it is such a wonderful way to go!!"

Betty's Bounty

"I have always had bountiful orgasms," writes Betty. This ageless sensual being, now approaching the seventh decade of her life, confesses, "I can remember having orgasms when in the sixth grade I would slide down a pole on the school's swing set during recess. I never thought it was wrong - in fact, I never thought of it other than a fun thing to do. I loved the feelings and assumed that every other girl in my class knew about those special feelings also. I was perhaps in the 4th grade when I first asked a girlfriend if she had these feelings 'down there.' I called them 'tinglies." I was surprised when my friend, looking somewhat bewildered, indicated that she had no idea what I was talking about! After discovering that this was not a common experience, my tinglies became my very special secret.

By the 6th grade, if not sooner, I discovered other ways to stir my tinglies. Humping a pillow worked. Rubbing myself with a plump stuffed teddybear worked. And, after a bit of practice, simply rubbing my clitoris with my fingers worked. By the time I was in junior high, I was masturbating daily. Orgasms were easy and multiple. My nightly ritual was to lie on my back with my pillow on my chest. I would caress a breast with my left hand, while stimulating my clit with my right. Being right-handed, I never succeeded in getting off with my left hand, so even if I switched back and forth, when the crucial moment approached, I would rely on my trusty right!

It was in my secret relationship with my pillow that I became aware that the fantasy of a girl lying on me was as exciting as imagining that it was a boy. I did not fully understand my bisexuality until much later in my life.

In the era in which I grew up, we were taught that although boys were sexual, they would not respect us if we gave into them. Nobody ever said that girls might have sexual feelings also and that these sexual feelings might be stirred by fantasies of both males and female. I periodically struggled with some guilt, but guilty or not, my tinglies felt so good I was not about to give them up. My first sex play was with another girl when we were both about 13. The sex play, which we engaged in many times, was really quite innocent and very superficial. Outwardly we each pretended the other was a boy, but I secretly enjoyed experiencing her as a girl and remember that she already had nice firm breasts that were somewhat larger than my own. I later learned that this girl went off to college, never married, and lived (closeted?) with another woman. I suspect as I was learning about my bisexuality, she was getting in touch with her lesbian nature. The second- and third-hand stories that reached me had a tragic side, as I heard through the grapevine that she had lost both her breasts to cancer. She did not win the battle and passed away a number of years ago. I would love to have been able to sit with her and exchange remembrances of our early sexual encounters. The naive exuberance and utter innocence of early exploration is too precious not to recall and share again with such special people.

My next encounter with a partner had to wait until I was 21 and ready to challenge the concept that sex must wait until marriage. My lover was a gentle man who, being atypical of men of that era, loved eating me. With him, climaxes were plentiful with manual stimulation, oral stimulation and (with practice and patience) with intercourse. We loved each others' orgasms. We loved the variety of ways we could get each other off. We parted friends - each with a bounty of memories of really fantastic sex.

My next two lovers were women. Sarah, the first, was one of the warmest people I have every met - warm emotionally that is. She felt in great depth and loved with great intensity. In bed she was a snuggler and enjoyed having her breast stroked, but Sarah was uncomfortable with touching or being touched in the genital area. I would lie beside her and masturbate - she would hold me, but not help me. We often cried together - me because I felt so incomplete, she because she felt so inhibited. We never resolved our sexual differences.

Pam was very different from Sarah. Pam was always busy, flitting around making work for herself. However, when she wanted sex, she threw herself into it completely. We quickly discovered the shared joy of '69ing.' We became so perfectly timed while giving to each other, we would orgasm in simultaneous explosions. Pam eventually went her own way, heading to the East Coast in search of the perfect job. We kept in touch by mail only briefly.

The next score of years brought a variety of partners, male and female, with periods of exclusivity interlaced with periods of promiscuity. A woman along the way introduced me to vibrators and, like everything else, these wonderful hummers produced countless numbers of orgasms. "Buzzing off" for quickies was great, and my trusty vibrators proved invaluable when I wanted to test the limits of my multiple orgasmic ability. Above all, however, I grew increasingly fond of oral sex.

I came to love the feelings of being licked and sucked, particularly when it was obvious that the person eating me loved doing it. To tell you the truth, I can not tell you if women were better at eating me than men, because I honestly believe that the loving art of cunnilingus is a skill possessed by both genders. I think the important characteristics of a good eater, regardless of gender, are their comfort with the concept, their acceptance of the responsibility, their admiration of the tastes, and their enthusiasm for giving.

I passed my 60th birthday several years ago and am still enjoying my orgasms almost as much as ever. I never married and never really felt too bad about that. I have known many wonderful lovers in my life and am now living with one of them - a very sweet old guy who has been impotent for years. He still likes to eat me from time to time, which I enjoy immensely. Usually, however, I get off now with my vibrator or during an occasional rendezvous with a very sensual old lesbian who can match me orgasm for orgasm. I liken myself to the old saying, 'There may be snow on the roof, but there is still fire in the furnace!' I hope for a long life and consider myself lucky to have experienced such a bounty of orgasms."

Brenda's Baptism

Brenda, being a bit shy, was initially reluctant to write down her thoughts about receiving oral sex, but once she got into it, she became quite open. She wrote, "I grew up in a very conservative home in which there was no mention of sex. I never masturbated, believing that it was wrong for girls to play with themselves. I tried not to have 'impure' thoughts and, for the most part, keep myself from feeling any 'immoral' desire. When that troublesome sexual yearning would hit (about once a month) I would feel guilty and busy myself until it passed.

I did not date much in high school and, when I did, I would break up just as soon as a boy began acting like he expected me to put out. When I look back, I realize I must have been seen as a real prude. I'm probably in the minority, remaining a virgin until I married at age 25.

Fred, my first husband, was a virgin also and, as I soon discovered, was very naive about sexual techniques. Our courtship had been fairly brief, only lasting 8 months. I think we both wanted to marry to be able to have sex without feeling guilty! We did our best as beginners, but we never could talk about what worked in bed and what didn't. However, we managed to continue our fairly boring sex life until the birth of Sandy, our first and only child. After that, something changed. I am not sure if I was responsible or if Fred was to blame, but we both stopped initiating sex. The time between our encounters stretched out to months and, when we did get around to 'doing it,' we were both nervous and self-conscious.

The last thing I thought I would ever do would be to have an affair. However, Fred not only stopped having sex with me, he also stopped talking to me. I was a full-time mother and he felt that he had to work long hours. I think he resented me for not working outside the home. Typically he would drag in late after work and ignore us. After eating dinner in silence, he would watch some sports on TV, and would inevitably fall asleep on the couch. Often he would not even bother coming to bed. I really did not miss sex with Fred, but I was bored silly and dying for some adult conversation.

The one luxury I allowed myself was riding my bike - both for exercise and for diversion. Three mornings a week I would drop Sandy off at my mother's house and join a small group of other bikers for a fast 10 mile ride along a city bike path. The group consisted of three other women and two men - all about my age (early 30's). We women jokingly called ourselves the 'Handlebar Hookers,' because 'we peddled our asses all over town!'

One of the two men, Kevin, was especially friendly and I found myself looking forward to our talks as we rode along the path. However, he then began calling me at home when Fred was at work. Usually we would talk for an hour or so, almost daily.

It was on one particularly cold wet morning that we decided not to ride. I invited Kevin to my house for coffee and, in anticipation of his visit, took Sandy to my mother's as usual. I know that I entertained the notion that we might kiss, as I brushed my teeth extra long and gargled twice before his scheduled arrival. I imagined, however, that it would only be a brief platonic kiss - *play* for him and *tonic* for me!

I was taken by surprise when, immediately upon closing the door, Kevin took me in his arms and kissed me passionately on the lips. I felt my knees buckle and his penis stiffen. I marveled at his immediate response. I don't think it was the kiss that did it - I think it was feeling him firming up - but I felt myself begin to get wet and my nipples engorged with excitement.

After that one long kiss and 'full body press,' Kevin backed off and started talking about the nasty weather. I became embarrassed and tried to hide my excitement (and erect nipples). I don't think I did a good job of concealing either my feelings or my nipples. However, I did begin to relax as we sat at the kitchen table exchanging small talk over a cup of coffee. Suddenly, and without announcement, Kevin got up and moved behind my chair. Bending over, he kissed me on the neck, sliding his hands around my sides and up onto my breasts. I thought my heart would break through the wall of my chest, it was pounding so hard. When I stood to face him he pressed his hard penis against my pubic bone and, with his hands on my buns, pulled me tight against him. I became light-headed and I felt my knees almost give way.

Things moved quickly from that point on, and within minutes we were on the living room floor. I began to shake uncontrollably, but Kevin calmed me with his voice and gentle touch. I remember little of his undressing me, except for the part where I lifted my hips slightly so that he could slide my panties down. I felt that I was ready for anything and everything, until he put his head between my legs. At that critical moment my Catholic guilt clicked into place and my legs automatically snapped closed!

Kevin seem undisturbed by my rejection of his oral favors and we went on to a marathon session of intercourse. We met several more times and each time he made a gesture that signaled he was about to head down to lick my genitals. Each time I closed my legs and pulled him up. Each time we moved on to intercourse. My physical passion began to change into emotional love and my expression of this seemed to make Kevin uneasy. I think he had problems with making a commitment, but he did not seem to mind having a purely sexual affair with me. He made it clear that he liked the sex, but did not want any emotional involvement. Between my nagging guilt and his lack of committed love, our intensity faded and we eventually drifted apart. We did not even bother to talk about ending our relationship - we just stopped seeing each other. I was hurt and guilty for a while and, I think, this was the beginning of my thinking about divorce.

I spent another year or so after my affair in my loveless marriage before I worked up the courage to confront Fred with my desire to divorce. He suddenly professed his undying love and went to great lengths trying everything he could think of in his last-ditch effort to save our marriage. However, I had emotionally turned a corner and his gestures were too little and too late. The marriage finally ended, with Fred still claiming he could not live without me. He never knew about my affair. It only would have made the ending worse.

Within a year of our divorce, Fred (who said he would die) married a younger woman with 2 children. I dated sparingly for a few years, not being sexual in any of these brief casual relationships. Working nights, caring for Sandy during the day, and fighting Fred for child support took most of my energy. When Sandy entered first grade I finally felt some relief. I changed to a day job and my mother (now a widow) volunteered to keep Sandy overnight twice each week. Every other weekend, Sandy stayed with Fred. As the pressure eased, I had time to think about myself and I began to miss the companionship of a man. With some single-again women friends I began to explore the singles' bars. I surprised myself by having casual sex with a few men, including at least two 'one-night stands.' Some of the men tried unsuccessfully to eat me, while others didn't bother. I successfully avoided it, having become skilled at closing my legs at precisely the right moment.

Eventually I burned out on the bar scene and began attending a singles and divorce group at a neighborhood Catholic church. I met John there. John was 7 years older than I, and an ex-priest. He had never married and had had very few sexual experiences. He was bright, caring and somehow very erotic. I felt a chemistry with John that I had never experienced before. His baldness and pot belly did not matter. I was intrigued from our first meeting.

We began to date initially as friends - meaning that we did not engage in any passionate kissing or other 'hanky-panky.' We talked of the meaning of life, shared stories of our religious experiences, and exchanged philosophies on everything from the death penalty to oral sex. We agreed on just about every political and theological issue of importance. Our values were almost identical. We seemed to be soul-mates - except when it came to oral sex! John knew that he loved both giving and receiving. As a result, he made it clear that he would not enter any long term relationship if it did not include the free exchange of oral stimulation. I felt that I had been thrown into the middle of a struggle between God Himself and the embodiment of Satan. The godly part of me said 'Keep your legs closed,' while the hedonistic part of me said, 'If you want John, you will have to give him what he wants.'

To make a long story short, I reluctantly allowed John to stimulate me orally and, once 'baptized,' I quickly grew to love it! I feel a little selfish because I have grown to be more comfortable receiving oral stimulation than I am giving it. However, John does not seem to mind, and I'll take all I can get! I have become a convert to oral sex and no longer worry that it is somehow wrong. We are married now and I feel especially close to John when he is pleasuring me orally. Together we feel blessed to have been created as sensual and sexual beings, and for this we give praise. We share the belief that God unconditionally approves of our physical and spiritual loving, regardless of how we choose to express it. We even feel that God understands our playful humor when we laugh about the baptism performed by my own very special 'Saint' John."

Exclusive Evelyn

Evelyn, now 45 years of age and the mother of two teenagers, said "My story is too boring." However, she agreed to tell of her experience with oral sex and, as you will discover, there is nothing boring about her tale. "I grew up thinking sex was a waste of time. I was always a good student, and, in my family, achievement was highly praised. Sex was a forbidden topic, other than the periodic lectures about the dangers of unwanted pregnancy. The prohibitions were not expressed as precautions to be taken to avoid the wrath of God, but rather as a practical plan to avoid roadblocks on the pathway to academic excellence. With the full backing of my parents, both of whom held Master's Degrees from prestigious Ivy League universities, I minimized my social life and maximized my study time. Dating held no real attraction for me, and I seemed not to miss the extracurricular activities that my peers felt were so important.

By about 15 I had become aware of sexual urges and it was almost by accident that I learned how to bring myself to orgasm without using my hands. I convinced myself that I was not being sexual if I laid on my stomach and rubbed myself on the bed. I would tighten all my muscles, bare down hard against the mattress, and concentrate on the feelings around my clitoris. Even though it was not direct stimulation, I could climax within a minute or two. There was never any sexual fantasy, never any imaginary partners, and never any erotic images. It was simply a quick physical release and an easy way to relax. It became my 'tranquilizer,' and, because it was a 'no hands' orgasm, I could do it with my sister sleeping in the bed next to mine.

Since sex was never really presented as 'dirty' or 'sinful,' I always viewed it as an option. The fact that I did not have any oral sex or intercourse until I was 23 was not because I felt that I would be damned to Hell. I simply had not meet anyone I chose to do it with! I did not have time and, if needed, I could get myself off quite swiftly.

Dave and I met after I had graduated from college. We taught in the same school district, although not the same school building. Dave and I knew each other very casually as colleagues for an entire school year before he asked me out. We actually had sex on that first 'official' date - each acknowledging that we had desired each other physically from our first meeting. I think it was a true case of 'lust at first sight,' but we quickly developed a deep and abiding love for each other. Furthermore, it was not long before we discovered that we were also the best of friends.

I did not orgasm with Dave on that first date, even though he tried everything (including oral sex). I remember feeling disappointed, but did my best to assure him that it was not his fault. During the next three or four months, I faked my orgasms so as not to upset Dave (who really was doing all that he could do). Even when he would spend the night, I would roll onto my stomach, tighten my muscles, grind subtlety on the mattress and experience my orgasm in silence. I did not think I had been detected during any of my personal quests for solitary relief.

One night, which I will never forget, as I began my quiet ritual (believing Dave to be asleep), I felt him move his body close to mine as he whisper 'I want to share this with you.' I was both embarrassed and excited by his awareness of what I was doing. I lost my edge, however, and could not finish. As I rolled onto my back, now feeling both embarrassed and frustrated, Dave moved directly down between my legs and began licking my clitoris. I had an enormous climax!

From that night when Dave first provided my 'tranquilizer,' I have had frequent and reliable orgasms while being eaten. We are now twenty years into our marriage and Dave remains the only man I have every made love with. Our sex life, though not frequent, remains novel, and, on the nights when our teenage girls are out, we find new places to share our sexual passion. We have made love in every room of the house, including the basement and the garage. We have made love in the back yard and in the back seat of our car while parked in our driveway. Oral sex has always worked best for getting me to climax and, for variety, I occasionally give Dave a 'blow job.'

We have tried as parents to present sex as a loving experience that one can share with someone who is really special. We try to teach the girls responsibility, without getting in the way of their responsiveness. Together, Dave and I have talked with them about masturbation as an acceptable physical outlet, but also as a pleasurable experience to be enjoyed. We have also been sure to allow the girls the privacy they need in their separate rooms.

My girls know about oral sex and, when the time comes for them to experiencing it, it is my hope that they can do so without restraint. Perhaps once they are adults and in their own sexual relationships, I will be able to tell them of my own enjoyment of cunnilingus with their father - my exclusive companion, friend and lover."

Lots for Lori

"Some who read this," Lori begins, "are going to think I'm a real slut! I began experimenting sexually at a very early age - by my self, with girl friends and with boys in my school. There were 'show and tell' sessions, as well as many episodes of 'playing doctor.' I put my fingers into every opening I could find on my body, and allowed my friends to do so also. There was never any abuse, for I always played willingly with kids of my own age. It's a wonder I was only caught once - that time being when I was about 6 and had taken my pants off in a tent set up in our back yard. My friend Bobby had just gotten down to inspect the mysterious structures between my legs when my mother opened the tent flap! I think she must have peed her pants! I ended up, after much scolding, being grounded for two weeks - confined to my room each night after dinner. I spent most of those boring nights playing with myself!

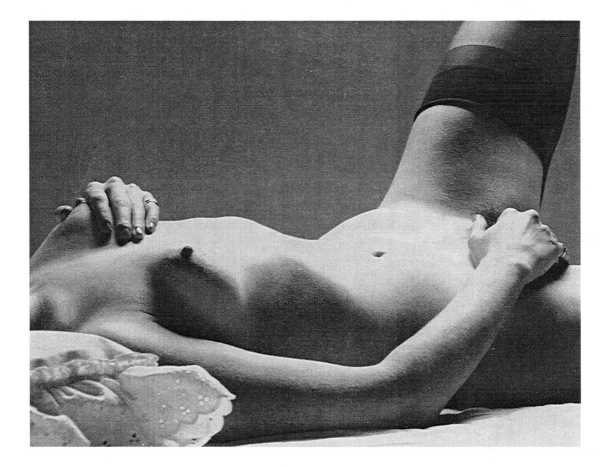

I lost my virginity to the handle on my hair brush by about 12. I began having intercourse with boys by 13, long before any of them ever thought to go down on me. I didn't know much about orgasms at 13, in part because boys that age do not know much about a girl's clit. Getting screwed felt good, but I was not cumming that way back then. When I was a kid, a boy showed me a picture book entitled 101 Positions of Intercourse. By 16, I had tried most every position of intercourse possible, including some that only a contortionist could duplicate. By now I have done all 101 positions - plus two that were not in the book!

I was 17 when a boy finally went down on me. I thought he was just going to kiss me and then come up again. Instead, he went at it like he really enjoyed it. In return, I went down on him, only to have him ejaculate immediately in my mouth. It was a wonderful introduction to oral sex - we were young, we were wild and we were horny. I loved it when he ate me and I thought nothing of swallowing his cum. I think we saw each other only once after that, but the details elude me now. I often try to remember his name and how we first met.

I know that there have been a lot of boys and men who's names I could not recall. If I thought about it, I could probably come up with a fairly accurate count of the nameless guys I have been with (at least while sober). Most of them were nice people, but I have slept with a few jerks along the way. I know I have been screwed in every position and eaten from every direction, but with every partner it seemed like a whole new experience. Different penises looked and felt different and different hands touched in different ways. Different mouths and tongues kiss differently - and feel different on my body.

I get off with some guys and not with others - the difference being their skill in giving head. Some guys are good, while others miss the mark - literally!

I think I'm good at giving head to guys (something I love to do with the nice guys, but refuse to do for the jerks). To me, oral sex is an art - I want to be considered an artist and, in return, love being eaten by a guy who has also developed the talent. I am more impressed by the way a guy eats me than I am by the way he screws. I try to remember the names of the few really good ones!

I'm not proud of my long list of men, for I feel that I have in some way used a lot of them. However, I'm not ashamed either. I have always tried to be up front with my expectations and have never promised more than I could deliver. I have experienced a lot and learned a lot and, at the ripe old age of 27, I am now ready to slow down a bit. The fear of AIDS has made me more cautious and I have entered an AA program to control my drinking and pot smoking. I'm not sure that I am ready to settle down with one man just yet, but I would like to sometime before I turn 35. I hope I will be able to be faithful - but I will not promise more than I feel I can deliver. It may be hard to focus on one man, after having had lots of variety. It seems important, however, for me to try."

Helen's Honey

Helen, a 29 year old woman from rural Wisconsin, recalls what for her was an eventful and very passionate high school romance. "I was 15 and felt that I was madly in love with Jerry, who was all of 16. It had not been too long since he got his first razor and it had just been a month since he received his driver's license. To us, in our young love and our burning lust, access to a car was our license to make out. No more petting on the front porch or living room couch. Jerry had wheels, and we were ready to get down to some heavy sex. We had both talked about oral sex and I openly shared my excitement about having him kiss me 'down there.' He had touched me with his fingers and he had looked excitedly between my legs to see my hidden treasures. We had even had intercourse a few times - real quickies on my living room couch with my parents asleep upstairs. With the car, however, new horizons of our sexuality were about to open up.

Jerry was eager as hell to lick me, but as we made plans to explore this new activity, he expressed some of his concerns. Basically, he was afraid I would smell and taste bad. It helps to understand Jerry if you know that at that time he was attending an all-boys Catholic academy, known locally as 'the seminary.' Everyone in town joked about all the semen that must flow there during the night, and in conversation 'seminary' often got changed to 'semenary.' In the sacred dorm and the secrecy of their rooms, the boys traded secrets about the mysteries of the female crotch, although I suspect few of them had had much real experience with a girl. Anyway, some of Jerry's friends at the academy had told him that girls taste like tuna!

When Jerry told me the tuna story I was initially shocked. I think for a few minutes I felt some shame, believing that what he said must be true. It seemed that I had heard similar descriptions. The punchline of a joke popped into my head - As Eve washed her crotch in a stream, God exclaimed, 'Darn, now I'll never get that smell out of my fish!'

I was lucky growing up. My mother did some things right, and one of these was to talk to me early and openly about my body, about my menstruation, and about my vaginal discharge. From the very first 'lecture' my mother gave, she emphasized the fact that there was nothing dirty or smelly about my genitals or the stuff that oozed out! I pushed back my shame and told Jerry I did not believe what boys said about girls smelling and tasting bad. In fact, I told him that I often touch my wetness and have tasted and smelled myself. 'Never have I smelled like fish' I exclaimed! I believed it, but Jerry remained leery.

I don't know how many people scheduled their first oral sex experience, but Jerry and I had a specific date set. We parked on the ridge outside of town - the local version of 'lover's lane.' After some heavy petting in the back seat, we were ready to do it!

I was really turned on and very much aware of having soaked my panties. Even with all my excitement and despite my positive thinking, I voiced my concerns about how I would taste. 'Never fear,' Jerry said to reassure me, 'Just lie back and relax.' He fumbled for a few moments and I thought he was opening up a pack of rubbers. I remember wondering, 'Is he going to eat me or fuck me?' I was surprised, however, to feel a thick syrupy liquid begin to drip onto my pussy. 'My secret sauce,' he joked, 'and it's going to make you taste even better!' Must have, for he licked it all up and drove me wild in the process.

Jerry refused to tell me what his 'secret sauce' was, but every time we parked he dripped it onto my clit, let it run down between my lips and eagerly licked it all out of my 'cunny!' He'd come up out of there with it in his hair and all over his face. Thus I uncovered the first clue to unraveling his secret when I planted a big kiss on one of his sticky cheeks. My suspicion was confirmed when I discovered an empty packet on the car floor - a packet of honey from the local fried chicken restaurant! To this day I can not put honey on a biscuit without laughing to myself as I remember that very sweet boy and those very sweet experiences we shared on the ridge."

Alice Finally Asks

"I've had sex with a lot of jerks," Alice begins. "I think I probably set myself up for some pretty nasty sexual experiences, since I somehow grew up believing that the surest way to a man's heart was through his dick! I'm sure that a lot guys saw me as an easy lie - but from my distorted perspective, every guy I got up and off was a sign of my sexual power. They may have thought that they were using me, but in my mind, I was using them. It was a real ego kick for me to feel a cock firm up in my mouth and then explode.

Most of the guys I was with had stronger sex drives than I did. I'm not into pain, and so on those occasions when I was not in the mood or could not get turned on, I could always avoid the discomfort of dry intercourse by offering either a hand job or a blow job. My offer was never turned down and a blow job was always preferred. It was not long before these selfish guys stopped asking me what I wanted and would simply ask, 'How about a blow job?' I would always oblige, and think I soon became an expert on giving good head. I was so quick to give, however, that I often ended up wanting to be loved on and pleasured by the guy who was now lying next to me, quivering and with his eyes rolled back in his head. But, each time I would put my own needs aside and rush to go down on a man, feeling this tremendous need to give him the most mind-crushing orgasm of his life.

Eventually I began to feel left out. Whenever someone would play with me or go down on me, and I had an opportunity to cum, I was rarely able to revel leisurely in the afterglow of my own orgasm. I would feel so damn obligated to return the favor that I would cut short my own pleasure in an effort to re-establish myself as the world's best 'cock-sucker.' Many nights I would end up feeling incomplete and unappreciated (not to mention, sexually frustrated). Sure, these jerks appreciated a fantastic blow job, but they did not seem to understand or appreciate that I needed some good sexual nurturing also. 'How about sucking me off?' became a request I heard frequently. I began saying to myself, as I dropped to my knees to take a hard penis into my mouth, 'No, how about you eating me?' I could never speak this out loud, fearing the man would reject me.

I was 28 when I met Chuck. He was 35 at the time and recently divorced. He had married young and had been faithful during the 14 years of his marriage. He claimed to have had a good sex life during the first 12 years of his marriage, but confessed that they had never engaged in oral sex. I was eager to introduce him to being on the receiving end of an expertly administered blow job, but he was initially reluctant. He expressed his curiosity about eating a woman, (and I expressed my eagerness to be eaten) but Chuck was not quick to offer it. As usual, I put my needs and desires on hold and proceeded to introduce this novice to the pleasures of receiving expert head.

It took a while to ease Chuck into being comfortable with my oral stimulation of his penis. When initially he seemed unable to cum this way I assumed it was because he was uncomfortable with this new stimulation. When it seemed apparent that he was not going to cum easily with my sucking, I doubled my efforts. My jaws would ache, but I continued to try - my reputation was at stake! We have now been together for three years and, to this day, Chuck has been unable to cum in my mouth. I had heard that some guys could not orgasm with oral sex, but I had never met one until Chuck came into my life.

I've grown to appreciate the fact that Chuck can lie back and allow me to suck on him, experiencing great pleasure in the process. I no longer feel that his inability to get off in my mouth is any reflection of my sexual ability. In fact, I have grown to feel that it is an advantage in our love-making, as I enjoy giving head without having to worry about swallowing. I get the best of both world - getting to enjoy pleasuring Chuck orally and then the pleasure of having him enter me.

As Chuck became more comfortable receiving oral stimulation he began to explore me with his mouth and tongue. My juice was like a magic potion, and I think he became hooked on eating me with the first lick of my pussy! Chuck is, in many ways, different from most of the guys I had known. He is more sexually playful, seems to be in less of a hurry, and is quite willing to give. Also, his sex drive seems less demanding than that of some other men I have known. In fact, my level of desire is somewhat higher than his.

One horny night I approached Chuck, hoping that he would be in the mood. He was willing to snuggle and kiss a bit, but I sensed no passion on his part. Realizing that he was not in the same place I was I backed off, feeling somewhat needy and disappointed. For some unknown reason, and without forethought, I blurted out, 'How about eating me?' Much to my surprise he did it! I have since learned that it is alright for me to ask to be pleasured and, although it is not every time, most often Chuck is more than willing to go down on me.

He has confessed that he feels some sense of sexual power in being able to bring me from dryness to wetness to orgasm and says that he feels he has become an expert at giving head. Sounds awfully familiar!!

The thing I have learned is that one should never *demand* attention from a partner, but if you don't *inquire*, you will never know if you can receive. I'm thankful that I was finally able to ask!"

Iᴛ's ᴛɪᴍᴇ ғᴏʀ ʏᴏᴜʀ ᴏʀᴀʟ ᴇxᴀᴍ

It is hoped that you have had a warm and receptive partner with you throughout your reading of this book, because it's time now for the final taste test! Put the book aside, but remember what you have learned.

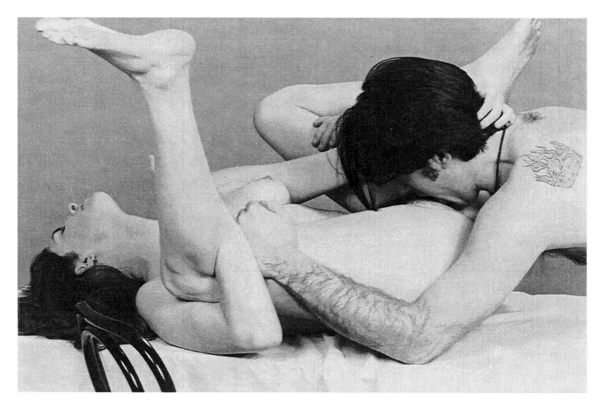

Good luck on your oral exam! BON APPETIT!!

RECOMMENDED READINGS

Akerley, B. (1985). <u>The X-Rated Bible</u>. Austin: American Atheist Press.

Barbach, L. (1975). <u>For Yourself.</u> New York: Doubleday & Company, and in paperback in 1976, Garden City: Anchor Press.

Douglas, N. & Slinger, P. (1979), <u>SEXUAL SECRETS: The Alchemy of Ecstasy</u>. New York: Destiny Books.

Dodson, B. ((1974). <u>Liberating Masturbation.</u> New York: Betty Dodson.

Eichel, E. & Nobile, P. (1992). <u>The Perfect Fit</u>. New York: Fine.

Ellenberg, D. & Bell, J. (1995). <u>Lovers for Life.</u> Santa Rosa: Aslan Publishing.

<u>Encyclopedia of Love & Sex.</u> (1972). New York: Crescent Books.

Heiman, J. & LoPiccolo, J. (1988). <u>Becoming Orgasmic</u> (Revised and expanded edition). New York: Prentice Hall Press.

Hite, S. (1976). <u>The Hite Report.</u> New York: Macmillan Publishing.

Horner, T. (1974). <u>Sex in the Bible.</u> London: Prentice Hall.

<u>Human Sexuality: New Directions in American Catholic Thought.</u> (1977).The Catholic Theological Society of America. New York: Paulist Press.

Hurwood, B. (Ed.). (1975). <u>Joys of Oral Love.</u> New York: Carlyle Communications, Inc.

Johnson, A., Wadsworth, J., Wellings, K., & Field, J. (1994) Sexual Attitudes and Lifestyles. Oxford: Blackwell Scientific Publications.

Kaplan. H. (1995). The Sexual Desire Disorders. New York: Brunner/Mazel.

Kinsey, A., Pomeroy, W., Martin, C. & Gebhard, P. (1953). Sexual Behavior in the Human Female. Philadelphia: W.B. Saunder Co.

Knopf, J. & Seiler, M. (1990). ISD: Inhibited Sexual Desire. New York: William Morrow and Company.

Ladas, A., Whipple, B., & Perry, J. (1982). The G SPOT: and Other Recent Discoveries about Human Sexuality. New York: Holt, Rinehart and Winston. Reprinted in paperback under same title in 1983 by Dell Publishing.

Larue, G. (1983). Sex and the Bible. Buffalo: Prometheus Books.

Lee, V. (1996). Soulful Sex. Berkeley: Conari Press.

Legman, G. (1969). Oragenitalism. New York: Julian Press. Reprinted under same title in 1979 by Bell Publishing and as a paperback under the title The Intimate Kiss in 1969 by Paperback Library.

Libby, R. (1993). Sex from Aah to Zipper. Grand Rapids: Playful Pleasure Press.

Michael, R., Gagnon, J., Laumann, E., & Kolata, G. (1994). Sex in America. Boston: Little, Brown and Company.

Morin, J. (1981). Anal Pleasure & Health, Burlinghame LA: Down there Press.

Ohanneson, J. (1983). <u>And They Felt No Shame</u>. Minneapolis: Winston Press.

Pelton, R. (1992). <u>Loony Sex Laws.</u> New York: Walker and Co.

Richter, A. (1987). <u>The Language of Sexuality.</u> Jefferson,NC: McFarland & Company

Ruan, F. (1991). <u>Sex in China</u>. New York: Plenum.

Sisley, E. (1977). <u>The Joy of Lesbian Sex</u>. New York: Crown Publishing.

Smith, R. (1992). <u>The Encyclopedia of Sexual Trivia.</u> New York: St. Martin's Press.

Stern, M. (1979). <u>Sex in the USSR</u>. New York: Times Books.

Stubbs, K.R. (1993). <u>The Clitoral Kiss</u>. Larkspur, CA: Secret Garden.

Wheat, E. & Wheat, G. (1981) <u>Intended for Pleasure</u>. Tarrytown,NY: Fleming H. Revell Company.

Wolfe, J. (1992). <u>What to do when HE has a Headache</u>. New York: Penguin Books.

Yaffe, M. & Fenwick, E. (1988). <u>Sexual Happiness for Women</u>. New York: Henry Holdt and Company.

RECOMMENDED RESOURCES

Adam & Eve, P.O. Box 800, Carrboro, NC 27510.

American Association of Sex Educators, Counselors and Therapists, P.O. Box 238, Mount Vernon, IA 52314

American Academy of Clinical Sexologists, 1929 18th St., N.W., Suite 1166, Washington, DC 20009

Astroglide, Bio-Film, 3121 Scott St., Vista, CA 92083

Eve's Garden, 119 West 57th St., Suite 420, New York, NY 10019

Femme Distribution, 588 Broadway, Suite 1110, New York, NY 10012

Focus International, 1160 East Jericho Turnpike, Suite 15, Huntington, NY 11743

Frederick's of Hollywood, P.O. Box 229, Hollywood, CA 90078

Gardener's Supply Company, 128 Interval Rd., Burlington, VT 05401

Good Vibrations, 938 Howard St., Suite 101, San Francisco, CA 94103

House O' Chicks, 2215R Market St. #813, San Francisco, CA 94114

Kessler Institute for Rehabilitation, 1199 Pleasant Valley Way, West Orange, NJ 07052

LIBIDO, The Journal of Sex and Sensibility, 5318 N. Paulina St., Chicago, IL 60640

Playboy Catalog, P.O. Box 809, Itasca, IL 60143

Sex over Forty, DKT International, P.O. Box 1600, Chapel Hill, NC
    27515

Sexuality Library, 938 Howard St., Suite 101, San Francisco, CA
    94103

Sinclair Institute, P.O. Box 8865, Chapel Hill, NC 27515

The Swing, 1298 South Virginia, Reno, NV 89502

Vermont Country Store, P.O. Box 3000, Manchester Center, VT
    05255

Vivid Video, Inc. 15127 Califa St., Van Nuys, CA 91411

Voyages, P.O. Box 78550, San Francisco, CA 94107

Note: Some of the video and sex toy companies may sell their mailing lists. Therefore, if you write to one that does, you might find yourself receiving mail from other establishments. Those who are not concerned about receiving explicit mail might enjoy this. Others might not. If you do not want on a variety of mailing lists, when you write or order, insist that your name not be sold. Most companies will respect this written request.

Photo credits

SEXISM STATEMENT
A. Photo by Carl Vogtmann, Figleaf Graphics

XXX EDUCATION
1. Courtesy of VIVID Video, Inc.*

THE EXPLORER'S MAP
2. PEC photo
3. PEC photo

IN SWEET ANTICIPATION
4. PEC photo
5. Courtesy of BioFilm, Inc.

HAIR TODAY, GONE TOMORROW
6. Photo by Pete Nitschke, Fantasy Boudoir Photography

FEATHERS, FUR, FANNIES, FANTASIES AND FUN
7. Photo by Pete Nitschke
8. Photo by Pete Nitschke
9. Photo by Pete Nitschke
10. Photo by Pete Nitschke

LUBRICATION, LATEX AND LINGUAL LUXUARY
11. Photo by Pete Nitschke

QUARTER MOON
12. Photo by Pete Nitschke

HALF MOON
13. Photo by Pete Nitschke

FULL MOON
    14. Photo by Pete Nitschke
    15. Courtesy of Ultimate/PHE, Inc.*

DON'T COME KNOCKING AT MY BACK DOOR!
    16. Photo by Pete Nitschke

THE "A" FRAME
    17. Photo by Pete Nitschke

STAND UP FOR WHAT YOU WANT
    18. Courtesy of Ultimate/PHE, Inc.*
    19. Courtesy of Ultimate/PHE, Inc.*

SITTING THIS ONE OUT
    20. PEC photo
    21. Courtesy of Ultimate/PHE,Inc.*
    22. Courtesy of Ultimate/PHE,Inc.*

TABLE THAT MOTION
    23. Photo by Pete Nitschke

SIDE-BY-SIDE 69
    24. Photo by Pete Nitschke

OVER-UNDER 69
    25. PEC photo
    26. Courtesy of VIVID/PHE, Inc.*
    27. Photo by Pete Nitschke
    28. Photo by Pete Nitschke

PEGGY'S PRETZEL
    29. Photo by Pete Nitschke

SIT ON MY FACE, PLEASE
    30. Courtesy of Ultimate/PHE, Inc.*
    31. Photo by Pete Nitschke
    32. Courtesy of VIVID Video, Inc.*
    33. PEC Photo

THE POPULAR FRONTAL ATTACK
    34. Photo by Pete Nitschke

A LITTLE HELP FROM A FRIEND
    35. PEC Photo (Dildos by Eve's Garden)

A TASTY TWIST
    36. Photo by Pete Nitschke

NIPPLES AND NOOKIE
    37. PEC photo

THE FLAT OUT LAIR
    38. Photo by Pete Nitschke

THE "T" FORMATION
    39. Photo by Pete Nitschke

MINDY'S MISERY
    40. Photo by Pete Nitschke

GETTING INTO THE SWING OF IT
    41. Courtesy of PHE, Inc.*
            From Nina Hartley's video <u>Guide ot Oral Sex</u>
    42. Courtesy of Bill Wilson*
            THE SWING, Reno, Nevada

THREE'S COMPANY
    43. Courtesy of VIVID Video, Inc.*

CLOSING THE CIRCLE
44. Courtesy of VIVID Video, Inc.*

AVOIDING THAT FALLOUT
45. Photo by Carl Vogtmann

Figleaf Graphics, Chicago, Illinois

FRAN'S FIRST AND FOREMOST
46. Photo by Elmer Batters

Cover Photo, LIBIDO, Fall 1995 Issue

SHARON'S SURPRISE
47. Photo by Pete Nitschke

BETTY'S BOUNTY
48. Photo by Pete Nitschke

LOTS FOR LORI
49. Photo by Pete Nitschke

HELEN'S HONEY
50. Photo by Elmer Batters

Photographed in 1970

IT'S TIME FOR YOUR ORAL EXAM
51. Photo by Pete Nitschke

* This photographic material is exempt from the requirements of 18 U. S.C. Section 2257 because this visual depiction of sexually explicit conduct was made prior to July 3, 1995.

PHOTOGRAPHIC RESOURCES

Carl Vogtmann, Photographer
FigLeaf Graphics
P.O. Box 11272
Chicago, IL 60611

A catalog of Carl Vogtmann's erotic fine art black and white photos is available for a nominal fee.

Elmer Batters, Photographer
P.O. Box 1707
San Pedro, CA 90731

1995 book of Elmer Batters' photographs entitled from the TIP of the TOES to the TOP of the HOSE, Published by Benedikt Taschen, ISBN 3-8228-9265-3

Pete Nitschke, Photographer
Fantasy Boudoir Photography
1195 West Fifth Ave.
Columbus, OH 43212

Specializing in the photography of loving couples and of the human form (bodyscapes).

PHE, Inc.
P.O. Box 800
Carrboro, NC 27510

Videos sold through the Adam & Eve catalog and include <u>Nina Hartley's Guide to Oral Sex</u> and productions by Ultimate and by Vivid Videos..

VIVID Video, Inc.
15127 Califa Street
Van Nuys, CA 91411

ABOUT THE AUTHOR

Dr. Bob Birch received his Ph.D. from the University of Wisconsin in 1967 and has been a psychologist for 30 years. After 10 years of experience in public mental health agencies, he went into private practice and began what is now a 20 year specialty in marital and sex therapy. He characterizes his professional interests as centering around intimate and caring physical and emotional relationships.

Dr. Birch is a Fellow of the American Academy of Family Psychology, a Fellow of the American Association for Marriage and Family Therapy, and a Clinical Fellow of the American Academy of Clinical Sexologists. He is a Diplomate of the American Board of Sexology and has been certified as a Sex Therapist and as a Sex Educator by the American Association of Sex Educators, Counselors and Therapists. He is also certified as a Family Therapist by the National Academy of Family Therapists. He is an adjunct assistant professor at the Ohio State University in Columbus, Ohio.

Dr. Birch has presented well over 300 public lectures and workshops and has written scores of articles. He has been interviewed multiple times on television, has been a regular guest on a late night call-in radio program, and has been quoted extensively in books and articles. Dr. Birch has dedicated his clinical skills, his public speaking, and his writing to the enhancement of sensuality and sexuality, believing in the importance of a solid physical and emotional bond in the maintenance of long term relationships.

Dr. Birch is in the private practice of marital and sex therapy and is the supervising psychologist at Beechwold Family Counseling Associated in Columbus, Ohio.